July 00

Dave,

Hope your Roman
dream comes true!

Love,
DSK

A GREAT WEEKEND IN

ROME

D0048164

Rome,

a unique city in every way

'The Past is the Present', as Lorenzo di Medici said. Of what city is this more true than Rome? Ancient monuments rub shoulders with new and Past and Present exist side by side in apparent harmony.

around Rome's ancient streets. The climate is warm and provides the perfect accompaniment for a spot of Latin sightseeing. You'll see that much of the city, down to the smallest side-street or secluded cloister, still retains a trace of the past as you venture past the doorway of a forgotten palazzo, hearing the play of water in the fountains. Time has been kind, the washed and faded ochres and reds blend so well with the deep green of umbrella pines under a brilliant Roman sky.

Rome is one of the world's most photogenic cities – not surprising when you remember what's here –

Of course, you won't be able to see everything in just a few days, there really is a such a wealth of things to do and see. Even the most minor church (unsurprisingly for the seat of the Catholic religion, Rome has the highest concentration of churches in the world) hides exceptional paintings, breathtaking ceiling frescoes and sculptures full of life. Don't worry, just take your time and enjoy strolling

SENSO UNICO

and clothing too, and very often at bargain prices, so that you can perfect your very own Latin look.

The Italians are also famous for taking the time to enjoy life – here you're never far from the next enticing *terrasse*, where you can stop for an espresso, a cappucino or a tiramisu. But if you are taken in by the provincial look of certain streets where tufts of grass grow between the paving stones, or by the sleepy rhythm of Rome at certain times of the day, then beware – you'll soon find yourself surrounded by a noisy merry-go-round of Vespas, cars and taxis, all honking their horns under the impassive gaze of marble statues. Don't forget though, you have been warned. 'The Past is the Present'.

The Vatican, the Trevi Fountain, St Peter's Square, the Spanish Steps, to name but a few of its famous monuments. Some will be familiar from postcards or school history books, but many more will not. There is a lot to learn for those who feel so inclined, but whether or not you spend your time sightseeing, or lazing in cafés watching the world go by, it will be your turn to feature in your very own *Roman Holiday*.

Though Rome may not be Italy's shopping capital, it nevertheless offers a wide selection of boutiques and other small shops where you'll find examples of the elegant yet casual Italian style. There are all kinds of tempting leather goods on offer, as well as knitwear, smartly designed items for the home and of course delicious culinary delights. The street markets are havens of tempting sights and smells, but if food is not your thing, they are often a good source for leather goods

If, at the end of your stay, the city has exerted its special brand of magic and you have thrown your coins in the Trevi Fountain and you want to return, Rome will always be there. After all, it is the Eternal City.

How to get there

Rome is a beautiful city at all times of the year but bear in mind the huge influx of visitors during Holy Week – unless of course you like crowds and are intent on seeing the Pope appear at his balcony.

WHEN TO GO

In August the Romans flee the heat and the city becomes calmer, though the temperature may also sap your energy. Remember too that many shops and businesses usually close for two or three weeks during this period. Consequently sales are held in July. It's also a period when many events are staged outdoors to take advantage of the warm Roman evenings. Autumn – from September to the end of October – has wonderful light and the temperature is ideal. November tends to be a rainy month. The good weather really starts as early as the end of April and the long, warm days in May are a delight, with gardens, balconies and terraces all starting to flower.

HOW TO GET THERE

For a great weekend in Rome, the best way to get there is probably by plane. From the UK and Ireland, the flight takes approximately two and a half hours. From the USA, Canada and Australasia, it is of course considerably longer and invariably requires a stop-over, although there are some direct flights (see details which follow). From continental Europe, the train is also an option, although probably only if you are going for more than a couple of days, since it might require a night on board. Details follow.

FLIGHTS FROM THE UK

There are several arlines offering flights to Rome and it is worthwhile scouring the back pages of the Sunday newspapers for cheap offers. Some of the airlines which fly direct include:

Alitalia
☎ 020 7602 111
www.alitalia.com
This website is packed with flight information and includes contact details for their offices worldwide.

British Airways
☎ 0345 222 111
www.british-airways.com
Flies direct to Rome.

Debonair
☎ 0541 500 300
www.debonair.com
An airline that generally offers good value for money, it is possible to find low fares here on flights from the UK.

Go!
☎ 0845 605 4321
www.go-fly.com
Owned by British Airways, this operator generally offers cheaper flights from the UK to European destinations, including 3 per day to Rome.

Virgin Express
☎ 0207 744 0004
www.virgin-express.com
Another relatively cheap option, their flights from the UK to Rome go via Brussels.

FROM IRELAND
There are operators offering direct flights to Rome, but you may be better off getting a cheap flight to London and continuing from there.

Aerlingus
☎ 01 886 8888
www.aerlingus.ie
Offers direct flights to Rome from Ireland.

Alitalia also fly from Ireland (www.alitalia.com, ☎ 01 677 5171 in Dublin) as do **British Airways** (www.british-airways.com, ☎ 01 800 626 747)

FROM THE USA AND CANADA
American Airlines
☎ 1 800 433 7300
www.americanairlines.com
Flies to Rome via London, Brussels or Zurich.

Air Canada
☎ 1 800 2687240
www.aircanada.ca
Flies to Rome via Frankfurt or London.

Alitalia flies direct from most US gateway cities and from Toronto and Montreal to Rome. Many airlines fly via other European cities, such as **British Airways** (www.british-airways.com, ☎ 1-800-AIRWAYS), which fly via London, **Air France** (www.airfrance.com, ☎ 1 800 237 2747), which go via Paris, and **KLM Royal Dutch Airlines/ Northwest Airlines** (www.klm.com, ☎ 1 800 225 2525), which go via Amsterdam.

FROM AUSTRALIA AND NEW ZEALAND

Flights from Australia and New Zealand are usually via Singapore or Bangkok, and in some instances, London.

Singapore Airlines
☎ 02 9350 0100 (Sydney)
www.singaporeair.com
They operate a daily service from Australia and New Zealand to Singapore. From there they have connecting flights to Rome three days per week. Call for more information.

Cathay Pacific
☎ 13 17 47 (free call)
www.cathaypacific.com
Fly daily from Sydney and Melbourne via Hong Kong.

Qantas
☎ 13 12 11 (free call)
www.qantas.com
Fly twice a week direct from Sydney to Rome.

British Airways
☎ 02 8904 8800
www.british-airways.com
Offers flights to Rome via London Heathrow. Visit their website or call them.

BY TRAIN

If you are already in Europe and are not in a great rush, the train is also an option, although you may find the prices are barely less than the cost of flying. In London, call:
European Rail
(www.europeanrail.co.uk,
☎ 020 7387 0444). They sell rail tickets for travel all over Europe and will send tickets out to UK addresses in advance. Ask about their discounted travel if you are under 26. You could try calling the **International Rail Centre** on
☎ 0990 848 848 (UK) or
Italian Railways on
☎ 020 7724 0011 (UK).

FROM THE AIRPORT TO THE CITY CENTRE BY TAXI

Rome has two airports : Fiumicino (also known as Leonardo da Vinci), which is 19 miles (30km) to the south-west, and Ciampino (for charter flights), 9 miles (15km) to the south-east. If you decide to take a taxi, use only the official taxis. The journey from the airport to the centre is fairly expensive (L60-70,000) and for only L10,000 extra you can hire a chauffeured air-conditioned limousine.

The number for chauffeur driven limousines in Rome is **Sater** ☎ 06 70 49 2812 Fax: 06 70 45 0388.

In Ireland, try calling **Brit Rail Ltd** on ☎ 01 661 2866/7 for information and reservations. From the USA, ask your travel

agent about train travel, or try browsing the **European Rail** website.

If you find yourself in France and want to go to Rome, it might be worthwhile visiting the **SNCF** website (French Railways), at www.sncf.fr (there is an option for an English version). In addition, this site has a page devoted to travel agents in Australia offering European train reservations. Or you could call direct for information in English (international number):
☎ (33) 836 35 35.

ITALY ON-LINE

There are hundreds of websites worldwide offering discount flights and other useful travel information – the web can be a very valuable source for travellers. We have put together a few suggestions:

www.expedia.msn.com
One of the busiest travel websites in the world, you can book a flight, reserve a room and rent a car on-line. Plus, includes links to Expedia sites worldwide – a good place to pick up lots of information.

www.deckchair.com
A UK-based website, this site will search literally millions of fares for the best-value flights available.

www.doit.it/en/
This site is packed with handy tourist and travel information and has links to other sites.

www.itwg.com
This site claims to have everything you will need to prepare for your trip to Italy.

SHORT BREAKS

Your travel agent will also offer copious short-break deals to Rome, offering flights and hotel accommodation in one package. It is worth seeing what is available from different tour operators, as you can sometimes save if you opt for a package deal.

FROM THE AIRPORT TO THE CITY CENTRE

From **Fiumicino** airport there is a direct train link to Termini station (the central station). If you alight at Ostiense station, a direct train will take you into the metro network (see map on inside back cover) at Piramide station. Tickets to Termini can be bought at the airport from ticket machines (L16,000) or at a counter (6am-11pm), where you can also buy bus and metro tickets, plus there are automatic ticket machines. The 64 bus leaves from in front of Termini

station and will drop you in Piazza Venezia, right in the heart of the city centre.

If you're arriving from **Ciampino** airport, take the bus service to Anagnina metro station, and from there travel to Termini station.

The Termini central train station is the hub of both the metro and the bus networks in Rome (and is best avoided late at night). In summer, the station is often crowded and you invariably have to queue at the counters, and at the exchange and tourist information offices. The station boasts an international telephone centre, a post office, a tobacconist's (for bus and metro tickets), a bar and a hairdresser's.

HEALTH & INSURANCE

No vaccinations are neccessary to go to Italy. EU citizens are entitled to health care, provided they are in

Importing and Exporting

In order to obtain authorisation to export an antique, you need to contact the Ministero dei Beni Culturali, Ufficio Esportazioni, Via Cernaia, 1 (Metro: Repubblica) ☎ 06 58 431, Mon., Wed. or Fri. before 11am. The procedure takes three days. Insurance cover is usually the responsibility of the company arranging transportation and is on the basis of the declared value of the item. Non-EU citizens should keep receipts for goods purchased in order to get a VAT rebate, providing they are exported unused and bought from a shop displaying a Tax Free sign.

possession of an E111 health form which covers basic medical expenses if you fall ill or are involved in accident (available from post offices in the UK). It is still advisable, however, to take out private travel insurance before you go to cover theft. Paying for your trip by credit card will often cover you for medical assistance and for baggage going astray, but you are advised to check with your credit card company to see exactly what is covered before you travel.

FORMALITIES

All EU citizens who travel to Italy must be in possession of a valid passport or identity card. All non-EU citizens must have a full passport – ensure it is valid before you travel! EU citizens and citizens of the USA, Canada, Australia and New Zealand do not need a visa for stays of up to three months. You are advised to make photcopies of all your papers, in case of an emergency. Beware pickpockets, keep your money safe in a money belt, and don't walk around with all your papers and all your money on your person. Police ☎ 112. Should you lose your papers, contact your embassy.

CUSTOMS

EU citizens do not need to declare any goods imported into or exported from Italy, providing they are for their own personal use. Non-EU citizens are allowed to import 400 cigarettes; 100 cigars; 200 cigarillos or 500gm/17oz of tobacco; 1 litre of spirits or 2 litres of wine and 50cl of perfume. In June 1999

duty-free sales were abolished between EU countries. Non-EU citizens may buy duty-free goods to export to their home country, but there are limits and your home country will have set allowances for the amount of goods you are allowed to import. Contact your local customs office for information:

U.S. Customs Service
☎ 202 927 6724

Revenue Canada
☎ 800 461 9999

Australian Customs Services
☎ 02 9213 2000

New Zealand Customs Services
☎ 09 359 6655

LOCAL CURRENCY
There are many tempting ways to spend your money in Rome. Buy Italian lire or traveller's cheques before you go and take your credit card. Banknotes come in denominations of 1000, 2000, 5000, 10,000, 50,000

and 100,000 L; coins come in 50, 100, 200, 500 and 1000 (also see p. 32).

LOCAL TIME
Italy is one hour ahead of Greenwich Meantime.

Summer time starts at the end of March, when the clocks are put forward one hour and winter time at the end of September, when the clocks go back one hour.

EMBASSIES
IN ROME

British Embassy
Via XX Settembre, 80a
☎ 06 482 5441

Irish Embassy
Piazza Campitelli, 3
☎ 06 697 9121

American Embassy
Via Vittorio Veneto, 119a-121
☎ 06 467 41

Canadian Embassy
Via G B de Rossi, 27
☎ 06 445 981

Australian Embassy
Via Alessandria, 215
☎ 06 852 721

New Zealand Embassy
Via Zara, 28
☎ 06 440 2928

LIFE IN ANCIENT ROME

Spectacle, debauchery and extravagance, each had a prescribed place in the daily life of Ancient Rome. The bloodthirsty circus games, the refined, but unusual, eating habits, and the importance given to personal appearance, were all governed by an unwritten social code. But as the gap between rich and poor widened, the sophistication and luxurious lifestyle enjoyed by the upper classes served to taunt and provoke the poor.

of events detailing the names of the gladiators, the weapons to be used, and what protection spectators could expect against the sun, e.g. parasols or sprayed perfumed water. The games would last all day and featured fights between wild animals or men, who were often dressed up to appear ridiculous. The afternoon attraction was the gladiators – either slaves or criminals – who had been trained in special academies. On occasion, some were even forced to take their own lives during the combats.

Quintilian, the 1st-century teacher of rhetoric, wrote down instructions for lawyers about how to prepare their togas the night before speaking in court. The story also goes that

there was once a Roman orator who wanted to take a colleague to court for simply having ruffled the pleats on his toga in a narrow alley.

THE SPECTACLE OF PAIN

Posters on the walls of the city announced the circus games, together with the programme

THE IMPORTANCE OF PLEATS

In Rome, the hang of the toga was considered as important as eloquence itself, and

THE ART OF MAKE-UP

Returning war heroes would march through the streets, their faces lightly made-up with an orange-tinted metallic pigment. This custom had its origins in a religious usage when, on certain festive occasions, the statues of the gods would be daubed with red paint. Pallor, on the other hand, was considered important for women, who used to smear their faces with

Gladiators before combat.

lead oxide (fatal, in the long-term) or crocodile dung in order to obtain a porcelain complexion.

TABLE MANNERS

Wine made from roses or violets would be served as an aperitif, and drunk from a single goblet as it was passed round. To liven up a dinner, dishes could be served in any order, and an unexpected dish was considered an agreeable surprise. The Romans were fond of culinary trompe l'oeil, to the extent that what appeared to be a fish could turn out to be chicken, and cheese could be prepared to look like a suckling pig.

A LIVING MENU

To allow guests to pick out the exact fish they wished to eat,

dining rooms were routinely set up alongside canals or swimming pools. Lucullus even had a dining room set up inside an enormous aviary, and to spare his guests from the summer heat, would receive them outdoors in a grotto built for that purpose.

THE LAWS ON LUXURY

The cost and duration of a banquet, as well as the number of guests that could be invited, were all subject to strict laws that Caesar enforced by posting guards around the marketplaces and ordering surprise house inspections. Certain luxurious practices, such as eating dormouse, were forbidden, and it was considered in poor taste to own over-expensive dishes (Vitellius was said to have owned a dish worth a million *sesterces*).

BLONDES HAVE MORE FUN

The complicated hairstyles of Roman ladies, as may be admired on the statuary in the Capitoline museum, were made from artificial hair. Customs documents of the time refer to hair imported from India, and we know a big market for wigs was held near the Circus Flaminius, where the blonde wigs that were all the rage at the beginning of the Empire were sold.

KNITWEAR AND DESIGNERS

The technique for knitwear dates back to the Middle Ages and was perfected during the Renaissance by gifted craftsmen who wanted to develop an elastic material for men to wear over their legs. The Italian knitwear industry has only really taken off in the last 35 years, and now its soft, warm, sensuous products are in demand all over the world.

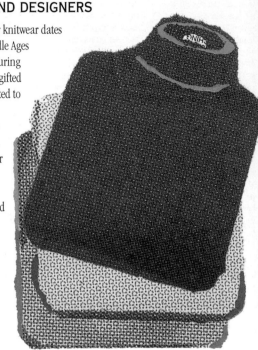

BACKGROUND INFORMATION

Every year Italy exports 550 million finished articles (sweaters, dresses, hosiery, scarves, gloves, socks, etc.), most of which are produced in the Emilia and Veneto regions. As there are not

enough Italian sheep to produce the quantity of wool required, most articles are made from wool shorn off the backs of Australian sheep. Europe's biggest importers of Italian woollen garments are Germany and England.

DIFFERENT TYPES OF WOOL

Lambswool comes from the first fleece of young lambs, and the best wool for making sweaters comes from eight-month old lambs. Lambswool is double-stitched and strong enough to be machine-washed. The wool from Merino sheep is very thin and malleable, and is used to make lingerie. Shetland wool is warm, hard-wearing and covered in a layer of fine down, and comes from the sheep of these islands. This type of wool produces a rougher and more rustic-looking finished product but gradually softens with use. Camel wool (or hair) is collected naturally, i.e. when

it falls off the animal, and is then retrieved, combed, cleaned, carded and spun. Angora is very fine rabbit hair (not to be confused with mohair, which comes from goats). Long, strong and with a sheen, it is used on

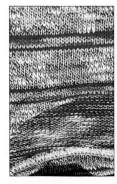

its own or combined in a mixture with another wool. *Paciumina* sheep are reared in the south of Italy and produce only small quantities (100-200gm/3.5-7oz per year) of the precious wool called cashmere, hence the high

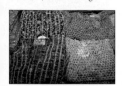

price. The wool is obtained by combing the animal in such a way as to separate the fine, soft hair (the part which is used) from the longer tougher hair.

KNITWEAR TECHNOLOGY

The Tremelloni library houses a collection of some 1,500 volumes and 95 journals dealing exclusively with the history and development of knitwear techniques. The tradition of knitwear in Italy is a very old one and modern day designers, such as Missoni, Benetton or Stefanel, have helped spread the style and colours of Italian knitwear all over the world.

ALL IN THE FINISH

The reason sweaters and other items of knitwear are often expensive is because the production process is long and sometimes complicated. Once the article has been knitted, it needs to be assembled and herein lies the art. In quality items the assembly is always made by hand and requires significant labour. And that's the only way to guarantee invisible seams.

WOOL CARE

As any knitwear expert will tell you, sweaters need to 'rest' after having been worn for a day, so the material

can regain its natural shape. In fact, Angora woollens should really be stored at cool temperatures, just like fur coats. You may want to brush your woollen garments from time to time to prevent small balls of wool from forming. And to keep off the moths, avoid using naphthalene. Use cedar wood instead, which is far less toxic.

There are no half measures in Italian knitwear: you have to choose between very expensive and often handmade articles, or more affordable mass-produced sweaters such as those by Benetton. Ottavio Missoni, the designer famous for his luxurious and stylish woollens, was the first to wear his own creations – at the Olympic games in London in 1948, when he was a finalist in the 400m hurdles.

THE BAROQUE STYLE: GRANDEUR AND MOVEMENT

The Swiss art historian H. Wolfflin put the onset of Italian Baroque at about the year 1580. Following on from the rigours of the Classical style, and the strict proportions of the Renaissance, the Baroque was typified by a taste for exuberance and embellishment. Roman Baroque is most clearly seen in architecture and the use of urban space, rather than in painting or sculpture. Its most famous exponents are Maderno, della Porta, Vignola, Bernini, Borromini and Michelangelo.

THE DOORWAY OF SAN ANDREA AL QUIRINALE

The Baroque introduced a sense of movement by concentrating all its visual effects on the central part of a building, in marked contrast to the Florentine Classical style, which created a uniform harmony without decorating doorways or windows. The church of San Andrea al Quirinale (see p.55) by Bernini with its heavily-adorned doorway is a typical example.

THE BALDACCHINO OF ST PETER'S

Art during the Renaissance sought to create permanence and so assume static forms. The Baroque, on the other hand, aimed for the opposite effect, and tended to use movement, especially movement upwards. This magnificent canopy in gilt-bronze dominating the nave and the main altar, where only the Pope can celebrate mass, was built by Bernini. It stands 20m/65ft high supported on four finely worked spiralling columns.

Church of San Carlo alle Quattro Fontane.

GAZE FOREVER UPWARDS

The interior of Baroque churches shows evidence of a new conception of space: the fixed forms of the past have given way to light, which suddenly appears to stream down from the height of the dome. But on the edge of the aisles, the side chapels remain in shadow, and the naked eye now sees cascades of clouds and bursts of light decorated with advancing angels where once there was only ceiling.

SHIFTS IN PROPORTION

The elegant proportions of the Renaissance were gradually abandoned in favour of heavier, less harmonious forms. The façades of buildings, as well as other architectural features (stairways, balustrades and windows), became wider, like the balustrade of the Capitoline stairway. Though the churches maintained their emphasis on vertical lines, cornices started to project and more horizontal decoration was used.

THE PALAZZI

Baroque churches and Baroque private residences were conceived along entirely different principles.

It's almost impossible to imagine that the same architect, Maderna, could have designed both the church of Santa Susana and the Palazzo Mattei which has

such a sinister appearance. Its austere façade gives no clues to the courtyard decorated with statues and busts. As was often the case at the time, an

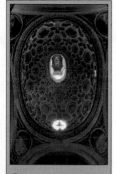

OVAL V. CIRCLE

The tendency of the Baroque style towards movement is best shown by its preference for the oval over the circle. The oval was used not only in stuccoed medallions, but also in designing floor plans, courtyards (San Ivea), cupolas (San Andrea), and even the pedestal of the equestrian statue of Marcus Aurelius on the Capitoline square.

uninviting, formal façade hides an interior full of artistic flourishes.

THE BAROQUE STYLE TODAY

The Baroque has continued to inspire artists and artisans, such as the painters of the *Transavanguardia* movement whose dynamic style of expression draws inspiration from the neo-Baroque. The designer Capucci has created cupola-style dresses, a clear reference to the architecture of the 17th century, and the jeweller Percossi-Papi is another artist who uses Baroque motifs in his creations.

Angel by Bernini, on Sant'Angelo bridge.

A LAND OF PLENTY

Italian cuisine – eaten in many forms in other countries – uses tasty, natural seasonal ingredients. The main dish, pasta, can be eaten with a range of basic Italian essentials – olive oil, herbs, ham, parmesan or mozzarella – and in combination with dozens of other ingredients. Now you're in Italy, try the real dishes for yourselves!

A COMPLICATED WORLD

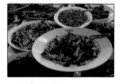

Rather like the plant world, which is divided into families, genera and species, pasta can be divided into fresh pasta, dry pasta or filled pasta, with or without eggs. All have poetic names: *capelli d'angelo* ('angel hair'), *orecchiette* ('little ears'), *conchiglie* ('small shells'), *rotellini* ('tiny wagon wheels') and *farfalle* ('butterflies') being a few examples. Guigiaro, the Fiat designer, has created a new type, the *marille*, but unfortunately these cannot be cooked properly as he has broken a golden rule – the *marille* are not all the same size.

THE 'KING' OF CHEESES

Reggiano parmesan has existed since ancient times, and is made from the milk of cows of Emilia-Romagna. It is sold by weight, and purists prefer to buy it cut in thin slices rather than grated. Reggiano should not be confused with the industrially-produced variety, the *padano*, or with the *pecorino romano*, a slightly spiced and very salty goat's cheese.

SWEET AND SOUR

Balsamic vinegar – which is quite expensive – has a distinctive and attractive dark brown colour and a very strong taste. It is a speciality of the Molise region and is made from the must of Trebbiano grapes, a vine of the Latium region, kept for a long time and matured for several years in gradually smaller barrels made of different woods (oak, chestnut, cherry, ash and mulberry). Balsamic vinegar is good for sore throats and the heart, and goes well with salads, meat and risottos.

HEALTHY OLIVE OIL

Italy's 180 million olive trees produce 624,200 tonnes of olive oil every year. These are graded by the EEC into different categories, according to acidity levels and the nature of the processing they have undergone. The best oil is called 'extra virgin' (*olio extra vergine di oliva*), and is pressed out of the olives at room temperature, just like a fruit juice; to be refined, it needs to be heated. If added to other olive oils, it becomes plain olive oil. If it's murky, i.e. unfiltered, it perishes more quickly, though the taste is just as good. For cooking purposes, Italians use a young olive oil, and for salads a lighter oil, which should be stored in a cool place away from light.

TASTY MOZZARELLA

The mozzarella produced in most dairies today is made with cow's milk and has little taste. By far the best type of mozzarella is the *mozzarella di Bufala* (made from buffalo milk), which owes its taste to

the briny nature of the pastures of Agro Pontino, an area of marshland to the south of Rome. This delicate cheese can't be kept long, and is delicious on pizzas, or eaten with tomatoes sprinkled with basil and topped with a trickle of olive oil.

A SMALL SLICE...

of ham. Norcia *prosciutto* is a salted mountain ham, which has a somewhat flattened

shape and is matured over six to eight months, during which time it's washed in red wine and spiced with garlic. Because it's stringy, it can't be cut with a slicer. Parma ham on the other hand is round, lightly salted, and matured over 10 months, which gives it its attractive pale pink colour. Don't forget to have it thinly sliced. The most sought-after and expensive hams (L50,000 per kilo/L22, 725 per lb) are Parma ham and San Daniele ham.

COFFEE AND CAFÉS

Who would have guessed that by signing the Continental System in 1806, Napoleon would become the inventor of the *espresso* – that small, extra strong black coffee? The Continental System restricted the consumption of colonial produce, and raised the price of coffee to such an extent that café-owners, no longer knowing what to boil in their coffee pots, used beans and chestnuts instead. This led to the idea that has since made so much money for the Caffè Greco (and others!) – reduce the size of cups by a third but serve them full of real coffee.

A LITERARY CAFÉ

The Caffè Greco, Via Condotti, 86 (see p.118) has lost none of its splendour since the days when it was a well-known meeting-place for intellectuals.

Casanova was one of the first to write about this café started by a Greek, and at the time the haunt of 'a bunch of gossips, pimps, castratos and abbots'. Proudhon, the French mid-19th-century political theorist, on the other hand, described it as a place to discuss painting and literature rather than scandal. You can make up your own mind.

SCHOOL FOR RIOTS

Cafés have always played an important role in the social and political life of Italy. During the reign of the popes, liberals would gather in them to criticise *sotto voce* the events of the day, whereas nowadays members of the government and opposition meet in them to trade insults and the occasional complicitous wink. And if there's an important football match on, then cafés become the scenes of epic occasions!

HOW TO DRINK IT

The famous 'black liquid' came to Italy from Constantinople via Venice. Today it is often taken standing at a crowded counter. It can be ordered as *espresso* (extra strong), *macchiato* (with a drop of milk), and either hot or cold. If served with a little more milk, it becomes a *cappuccino* –

a latter-day symbol of Italy – and when served with chocolate, it becomes *mischio*. An equal proportion of coffee and milk produces *caffelatte*. Coffee is served in a cup or small glass (*bicchierino*). In winter it can be taken away in a thermos and in summer can be drunk as a *granita*, i.e. on ice, or simply *freddo*, cold. If taken without sugar, it is *amaro*. And for the above you need a shining, gleaming, whistling, sighing, animated chrome sculpture – the Italian coffee machine.

COFFEE WITH A DIFFERENCE

Unlike homemade coffee, the *espresso* served in cafés contains oils and colloids, which cause the coffee to froth more and help it to enter the taste-buds. In cafés, coffee is prepared using water at a temperature of 90°C (162°F) at great pressure, whereas in the percolator in your kitchen the water is at 100°C (212°F) and at lower pressure, hence the difference in taste. Furthermore, the thick porcelain cups are shaped to allow the aroma to disperse freely before you've even had a sip.

ETIQUETTE

A place to talk politics or literature, a place to meet friends or a backdrop to

IT COULD BE YOU!

According to a custom that originated in Naples and which, apparently, is still practised today, a generous benefactor may pay the barman in advance for a certain number of coffees to be offered to the less well-off clients at the barman's discretion.

amorous affairs (though women were not admitted until the mid-17th century), the café is many things. Nevertheless, there are certain rules: always pay in advance, never leave your bag unattended, and only leave a tip at your discretion. Though the telephone may not always work, the toilets are usually open and some-times have an attendant to help spruce you up. And on Sundays, when everywhere else is closed, this is where you can buy mineral water, milk and wine.

PRACTICALITIES

You'll find Rome's cafés open early and close late. They're wonderful places to quench your thirst, have a bite to eat and feel part of Roman daily life.

ITALIAN DESIGN

Italian design has its roots in the artisan-craftsman tradition and a thriving artistic culture. It flourished for the first time at the end of the 1950s when Giocosa designed the Cinquecento for Fiat, and Ascanio, previously known for his helicopter designs, created the Vespa which went on to make a fortune for the manufacturer Piaggio. And since the 1970s a real creative fervour made Italy a leading light of contemporary design.

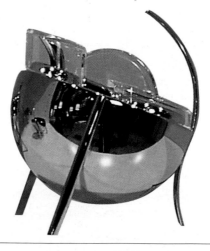

BACK TO EARTH

After the excesses of the 1980s, the 1990s saw a return to more down-to-earth lifestyles, and with them the return of wood, which quelled the fad for metal and gadgets. The new generation of designers have sought inspiration from the craft industry and used it to create a more sober style of industrial design reminiscent of simple, traditional forms. It's a more subdued approach fully in keeping with a renewed emphasis on natural materials and authenticity.

FUTURISTS MATERIALS

In Rome, you'll find a good sample of new fashions and a wide choice of ultramodern objects and furniture. Traditional materials are once again popular, but composite materials invented for the aerospace or aeronautics industry are now also widely-used. Italian designers were the first to take advantage of new materials such as titanium, which is stronger yet lighter than steel, and carbon fibre, used to reduce the weight of furniture (particularly chairs) and improve durability.

GREEN FASHION

The use of new materials coincided with the spread of recycling methods. And since they contain polyester fibre, 350 million mineral water bottles can now be converted every year into chairs or armchairs. The most famous chair of its generation is called *Seaweed* and was designed by Gaetano Pesce. The shoe company Superga made the *Relife* basketball boot from recycled materials, and *Greenwatch* is the first Italian watch to use recycled products in its manufacture, which includes 25 different types of plastic. Technology nowadays uses composite products that are continuing to blur the distinction between what is natural and what is purely man-made.

ALESSI

With a constant desire for innovation, Alberto Alessi has developed his tableware business into a leading light of fashion and contemporary design. After hiring the talents of big names in design to create saucepans, coffee pots and dinner services, such as Philippe Starck who designed the *Ti Tang* teapot (about L400,000), he hired new names like Andrea Castiglioni and Carla Ceccariglia to create amusing and original stainless steel objects.

MANUFACTURERS AND FAMOUS OBJECTS

Modern Italian furniture designers like Cappellini, De Padova, Matteograssi, Kartell and Saporiti are now world famous names. For those of you interested in light fittings, Arflex, Artemide, Mazzega, La Murrina, and Flos all offer an enormous choice using the latest technology for both the materials and the electrical system. The *Filiberto* sofa, which

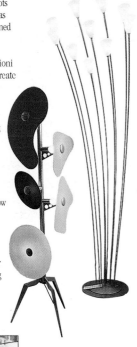

you can find in Magazzini Forma e Memoria, was designed for Flexiform by Citterio, as was the *M2059* teak table with zinc legs, for sale in Cappellini. And if you're looking for elegant and lightweight presents, we should add Tonucci, who makes leather and wood objects.

> '*We want to be able to design objects that have a role in our lives, and that have a sense of humour or a sense of the tragic. Over the years, we designers have discovered ways of communicating succinctly. And we want to use this vocabulary, which is derived not from the marketplace but from life.*'
>
> **Ettore Sotsass**, the pope of 1980s Italian design.

GLOVES, SHOES AND HANDBAGS

The Maremma is an uncultivated region between Rome and Florence still ruled over by the herdsmen (*butteri*) who raise cattle and horses there. In the past, these Italian cowboys made tools and workwear – boots, harnesses and shoulder bags, but nowadays, the region's craftsmen specialise in hand-stitched fine leather articles.

GUCCI

Guccio Gucci opened his first shop in 1922. It sold leather

goods and elegant sportswear that was popular with the Italian jet set of the period. The business expanded in the 1960s, and today the boutique in Via Condotti is an obligatory port of call for Hollywood and Cinecittà film stars, who all come to try on the latest shoes or the *Flora* neckscarf created for Grace Kelly in 1966. Updated 1960s designs have also formed part of recent Gucci creations.

THE IDEAL SHOE

At the beginning of the century, Salvatore Ferragamo was a man with a passion for his work making handmade shoes for individual clients. After studying the anatomy of the foot at university, he made his reputation with a support for the sole of the foot. Soon his shoes became known for being both light and comfortable, i.e. he

SECRETS OF A GOOD SHINE

According to tradition, you need to expose your shoes to moonlight if you want different colours and degrees of transparency in the shine of the leather. In actual fact, different tints can be obtained by rubbing dark blue polish into light-coloured leathers,

and for a really polished black shine, you can add a small amount of red. If you want to retain the natural colour of untreated leather shoes, wash them with a specially-designed leather soap and then coat them with Nivea cream. Allow the cream to be absorbed, then shine with a natural-coloured polish. Always use silicone-free products.

squared the circle. 'A good shoemaker is able to make shoes narrow on the outside but wide on the inside', as Italy's great comic actor Toto used to say, and Ferragamo's shoes are exactly that.

TANNING

The Italians are well-known for their tanning of leather, which is normally done over 15 to 20 days using pieces of bark. Chrome treatment makes the leather softer and more resistant, whilst animal oils are used in the treatment of kidskin and calfskin. The colours used depend to an extent on current fashions, though certain classic tints are always popular – black, white and brown.

TOD'S SHOES

As the years have gone by, the success of this relatively recent brand has achieved mythic proportions and 1.3 million pairs were sold in 1995. Diego della Valle, the son of a shoemaker, designed the first pair of Tod's in 1979 and hasn't changed them since. The shoes, produced in the family-run factory in the Marche region, always bear the T logo with the lion's head – the stamp of authenticity.

GLOVES, THE FINISHING TOUCH

Gloves are back in fashion and are used not only to accessorise a style but sometimes also to add a flourish. Most glovers are based in Naples, perhaps due to the softer water there, a key requirement in the process of the washing and tanning of leather. On average, a pair of gloves requires two and a half hours of labour, carried out in a total of 86 stages.

A WELL-MADE HANDBAG

When it comes to assembling the various pieces, the key factor is the dosage of glue, not the type of leather (whether calfskin, kidskin or ostrich). To find out if the work has been well done, run

your finger along the seams to see if they are completely regular. In theory, any extra leather should have been carefully removed by hand and the stitching should be quite undetectable. This smoothness is the mark of a skilled worker.

THE FASHION INDUSTRY

Whilst Milan is the ready-to-wear fashion capital, and Florence the centre for men's fashion, Rome is the capital of haute couture. Some of its couture houses are already world famous – Valentino, Versace and Armani – and there are others – Brioni and Gattinoni – who have yet to be discovered. All have tried to widen their renown by creating ready-to-wear collections, as well as jeans and lines of accessories. All have employed other talented designers. Here's a little background to the world of Roman fashion.

THE ARISTOCRATS OF FASHION

Nowadays, key figures such as Ferragamo, Fendi, Gucci, Armani and Missoni live just like the great patrons of the arts at the time of the Renaissance. They form links with the richest families, buy the most beautiful palazzi (and have them restored by the best craftsmen) and spread the Italian look all over the world.

RISING STARS

Roberto Capucci's sense of style has given birth to such ideas as dress-sculptures in the form of cupolas and draws inspiration from Baroque and trompe-l'oeil designs. His creations are now found in important museums around the world, including the MET in New York and the Uffizi in Florence. Another designer who loves Rome, and especially the Vatican, is Gattinoni, though no-one could describe his dress-cassocks as orthodox.

PROVOCATIVE MARKETING

The 'Energie' label will do anything to appeal to its appreciative young customers, from window displays showing scenes of destruction to pictures of the Pope in blood – stained robes enthroned on an enormous pile of trashed jeans. Italians love risqué adverts – such as those by one

particular designer showing six positions of a man's penis under his jeans.

THE RETRO LOOK

The designers working under the label Rocco Barocco draw their inspiration from films and the 1950s – a period when the eccentric prince, Dado Ruspoli, would stroll about Capri with a chicken on a leash. These are designers who love to provoke and use daring designs and mixtures of styles. Their favourite model is Mussolini's young grand-daughter Rachele.

STYLE FOR ALL

Egon von Furstenberg, the grandson of Gianni Agnelli, has a Baroque, over the top style, popular with wealthy young women. He does,

however, also target the average consumer, as his designs can be found in mail-order catalogues. Von Furstenberg has also created a collection for sale in the Metro and Upim supermarket chains.

THE BUTTON KING

Gai Mattiolo loves buttons. His ladies' suits are covered in them – though happily not all are the type of button that needs undoing. He designs his own accessories and then commissions their manufacture from artisans. Some of his most regular clients are famous female TV personalities.

READY-TO-COPY

Rome is also the counterfeit capital. The *prontisti* (as these almost official counterfeiters are known) are the sworn enemies of the designers. This is hardly surprising when you discover that Halfon, Ferrone, and Max Dine, the kings of *pronta moda*, can sell a pair of good-quality

THE ORIGIN OF JEANS AND DENIM

The famous cotton cloth from Gênes (in France) – hence 'jeans' – is thought to have been in existence since 1567. At that time, it was used as a backcloth to the building work around the Holy Sepulchre during Easter week. Peasants from Gênes then brought it to Nice and from there it spread to Nîmes – hence the name 'de-nim' (de Nîmes, meaning 'from Nîmes) which the Americans used to designate this type of cloth.

Armani-style trousers for as little as L20,000. Their goods are sold under the brand name Altra Moda.

GARDENS, TERRACES AND BALCONIES

After having discovered the remains of Hadrian's Villa and works by Pliny during the Renaissance, it became the turn of the Popes to commission villas, once the prerogative of the patrician families of Ancient Rome. All along the banks of the Tiber, from Rome to the coast, many villas and gardens were built overlooking the hills. Today the same taste for *villeggiatura* can be seen in Rome itself, with sumptuous terraces housed specially on rooftops, a favourite location for social gatherings in the summer.

METAPHYSICAL GARDENS

The Dream of Poliphilus came out in 1499 and became the guidebook to Renaissance gardens. At the time, architects wanted to give a new meaning to the natural world and they drew inspiration from the text, seeing the garden as the first step into a fantastical world. The labyrinth became the symbol of this new style of garden aimed at arousing both the mind and the senses.

VILLA GARDENS

A perfect example of the Renaissance city palazzo is Villa Farnesina in the

Trastevere quarter of the city. With its wide, well-lit gallery and salons, and a loggia overlooking the Tiber, it was ideal for receiving guests and enjoying the pleasures of conviviality to the full. Up amidst the extensive greenery of the gardens of Villa Borghese is Villa Medici, the wonderful gardens of which can be glimpsed but unfortunately are not open to the public (though have a look at the façade).

HANGING GARDENS OF ROME

You'll find not only geraniums on Roman terraces, but also cypresses, pine trees, palm trees (in Via Lata) and even giant cacti. Wild rocket often sprouts up between the roof-tiles and basil is grown in

window boxes. Roman terraces may not quite be suspended between heaven and earth like the hanging gardens of Babylon, but they do appear to defy gravity.

> ### A MICROCOSM OF NATURE
>
> '*Villa Borghese. An extensive park with wild animals, ponds and fountains, a riding school, copses, flower and vegetable gardens, aviaries, an orangery and a labyrinth - in other words, all that man can create from nature.*'
> Mme Du Boccage, *Letters, 1771.*

THE HOLY BALCONY

Every Easter day, thousands of pilgrims gather on St Peter's Square to receive the papal blessing '*urbi et orbi*' (to Rome and the world). This is the only time the Pope appears at this balcony. For the Sunday

blessing, he addresses the faithful from the window of the Vatican palace.

COOL BOTANIC SHADE

In the heart of Trastevere, near the Farnesina palace, are the shaded paths of the botanical garden. It's a peaceful and romantic place known mainly to the local residents. And there's nowhere like it in central Rome (Largo Cristina di Svezia, 24, Mon.-Fri. 8am-6pm, Sat. 8am-noon).

NEW YEAR'S EVE

On the night of New Year's Eve, it's never easy to find a table on the terraces, which offer the best views of the firework displays held every year to celebrate the New Year. It used to be the custom to throw all unwanted objects

out of the window so that they crashed onto the street with the loudest possible noise and kept away evil spirits. During the year, people would stockpile empty bottles and old light bulbs in preparation for

the occasion. Luckily they've stopped that in Rome, though watch out if you're going down to Naples.

WATER, WATER, EVERYWHERE...

Rome has some of the loveliest and most exuberant fountains in the world. Many were commissioned by popes aiming to stamp their mark on the city, but as long ago as the 4th century some 1,352 fountains, and 14 aqueducts could be counted. Running water was plentiful and furthered the development of public baths and right up until the 19th century, it was water that protected the city from cholera. Nowadays, Roman fountains consume some 2,000 litres/528 gallons per second.

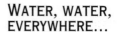

NAVAL GAMES

Aquatic entertainment was highly appreciated in Ancient

Rome and people came from all over to watch spectacular naval battles staged on artificial lakes and involving real or almost life-sized boats. The Emperor Claudius brought in 100 warships and 19,000 men for such recreations. And the Emperor

Augustus had a 33km/21 mile aqueduct built to fill a huge 200,000m^3 pool, as well as a canal linking the pool with the Tiber. In the end however, the stagnant water caused outbreaks of malaria and the arena had to be destroyed.

THE TIBER

Rome's small river is almost 400 km/249 miles long and

has its source in the Apennines. It is nothing like the great rivers that flow through the capitals of northern Europe. Most of the year, the water level is very low and its banks are covered in wild grass. Nevertheless, 19th-century drawings do show houses standing in water. Marble plaques still indicate the levels reached by the

deadly floods which have wreaked havoc throughout Rome's history. It was to give thanks for the drop in floodwater levels that Bernini's father built the fountain in Piazza di Spagna. Finally, in 1870, Rome began to put in place huge embankments along both sides of the river to control excesses.

THE SANT'ANGELO BRIDGE

This bridge was first built in AD 134 by the Emperor Hadrian to link his mausoleum with the right bank of the river, and has been modified several times since. In 1667, Pope Clement IX commissioned Bernini to create 10 white marble angels, each bearing an object from the crucifixion of Christ (e.g.

nails, cross and crown of thorns). The angels were in fact completed a year later by pupils of the great artist. When seen at around 5pm from Via dei Banchi Vecchi, they appear to turn red in the light of the setting sun, like a vision of religious ecstasy.

ACQUA VERGINE: A MAGIC AQUEDUCT

Aqueducts were constructed to bring in a constant supply of water from the surrounding hills – some were as much as 80 km/50 miles long. One of the most famous is Acqua Vergine, an underground aqueduct and the only one to have survived the invasion of Rome by the barbarians after the fall of the Empire. This is the aqueduct that feeds the Trevi Fountain, as well as those in Piazza Navona and on the Capitol, and is open to the public. Its water is said to have healing powers, such that the aristocracy used to take some on their travels as a protection against sore throats.

CAN YOU DRINK THE WATER?

Water in fountains, and in some cases running water, is *non potabile*, i.e. not for drinking. Some apartments still receive water carried by ancient aqueducts such as the one from the

> ### WATER FOR MIRACLES
>
> In accordance with popular belief, on the day of St Laurence, many women who are sterile go to drink the water from the well of the church of San Lorenzo in Lucina (right by Piazza di Spagna) in the hope of becoming mothers.

Abbruzzi region (to the east of Rome), built in AD 52. However water in the fountains between Campo dei Fiori and the Janiculum is perfectly drinkable.

The Boat Fountain, Piazza di Spagna.

Rome – practicalities

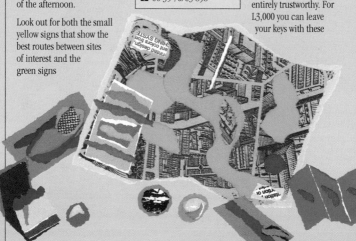

GETTING ROUND THE CITY

The historic centre is not particularly large (only 2.5 km/1.5 miles from the Colosseum to Piazza di Spagna) and so is easy to visit on foot, particularly as most monuments are to be found in the same area. Walking is also the best way to explore the city and allows you to make your own programme of visits with shopping or stops along the way for refreshment. Unfortunately, Rome's few pedestrian streets are often overrun with bikes and scooters. If you go in summer, you'll soon see the appeal of the famous Roman *farniente* (doing nothing) when the sun's at its hottest. And what better place than a shaded terrace alongside a fountain for that? In any case, churches and most shops are usually closed until the end of the afternoon.

Look out for both the small yellow signs that show the best routes between sites of interest and the green signs

indicating the best route to follow for major monuments. It's worth mentioning that, even when you're crossing roads where you think you have the right of way, Roman drivers won't always respect it. And if you're driving, expect to hear horns and to be overtaken on both sides. That, together with the bravado of the scooters and other two-wheelers (it's not unknown to encounter them driving on

the wrong side of the road), and the nonchalance of certain pedestrians, means you'll find it hard to keep calm at the wheel. Not to mention the maze of one-way streets in the city centre. You'll soon see why the Italians never stay calm for very long. Parking within the historic centre is reserved for resident permit-holders, so if your hotel doesn't have space for vehicles, you may need to resort to the car park under Villa Borghese. However, be sure to lock the car and not to leave anything of value visible inside. Otherwise, there are unofficial car parks, and though they may not always look it, the attendants are entirely trustworthy. For L3,000 you can leave your keys with these

TAXIS

Taxis are expensive but also convenient if you have heavy luggage. Always take the official (yellow) taxis. They can also be hired by telephone:
Cosmos Radio Taxi,
☎ 06 88 177
Società la Capitale,
☎ 06 49 94
Radio Taxi,
☎ 06 35 70/63 898

parcheggiatori, and they'll give you a receipt and look after your car for several hours. Apart from theft, the other risks you could face at night are traffic lights flashing orange (they are switched to this mode late at night and it is up to you to decide when or whether to cross!), and the effects of drinking too much Chianti!

Finally, if none of the above puts you off, you could always avoid the traffic jams by renting a moped. Helmets aren't obligatory, but your credit card number will be required as a guarantee. Most agencies are closed on Sundays.

Scoot-a-long, Via Cavour, 302, ☎ 06 678 0206.
St Peter Moto, Via di Porta Castelo 43, ☎ 06 687 5714 or
Telephone Hire Service, Lungotevere Marzio 3 ☎ 06 68 80 3394.

BY BUS AND TRAM

If you ask at the ATAC booths in Piazza del Risorgimento, ☎ 06 46 95 4444, or in Piazza dei Cinquecento, outside Termini Station, you'll be given a detailed map of the public transport network. ATAC is the city transport authority.

Tickets can be bought in kiosks, tobacconists, and metro stations. It's better to buy them in advance as ticket machines are often not working, and don't always have change. Tickets cost L1,500 and are valid for up to 75 minutes after they have been validated. During this time, they can be used to make several bus journeys (no need to validate them

again), as well as a single journey by metro. Most buses and trams run from 5.30am to midnight. There is also a night service (indicated by an N) serving the city centre and surroundings. Bus stops (look for '*Fermata*') have a yellow sign showing several route numbers that you should find detailed below. Route 64 has been completely modernised recently and now leaves at two to three minute intervals. It's as reliable as the metro with the added advantage that it crosses the historic centre to link St Peter's and the central station. The new (electric) 116 bus also crosses the historic centre (leaving near the church of San Giovanni dei Fiorentini), and passes Palazzo Farnese before ascending to Villa Borghese.

And for the romantics among you, there are the horse-drawn carriages to be found stationed around St Peter's Square, Piazza Venezia, Piazza di Spagna, Piazza Navona, the Trevi Fountain and Via Veneto (agree a price before you set off).

BY METRO

COTRAL runs the metro system. The Roman metro goes round rather than through the historic centre. It only has two lines, which intersect at Termini central station.

It is a relatively recent addition to the city, and though already covered in graffiti, is in parts not completely finished.

WRITING HOME

If, despite the legendary slowness of the Italian postal network (a month to reach

another European city during August), you still want to send postcards, you can buy your stamps (*francobolli*) at the tobacconist's or a post office. The main post office is in Piazza S. Silvestro, and is perhaps the only place to buy collector's stamps (Mon. to Fri., 8.30am-7.30pm, Sat., 8.30am-11.50am, and mornings only for collector's stamps). Letterboxes for mail going to foreign destinations are either sky blue (with the European Union stars) in the historic centre, or red, with a slot for destinations outside Rome. Official statistics show the first option is the fastest. Note too that the Vatican State has its own separate postal service and stamps. Its letterboxes are also blue and are to be found around St Peter's Square and the Vatican museums. Be sure not to mix them up, as Italian stamps cannot be used in the Vatican and vice versa.

MAKING A TELEPHONE CALL

You can make phone calls from any of the numerous telephone offices (*telefoni*), where an operator will assign you to a booth and the meter will start counting as soon as you get through to your destination. The office in Palazzo delle Poste, Piazza San Silvestro, is open 24 hrs a day. The orange SIP public telephones accept (L100, L200 and L500) coins or telephone cards (L5,000 or L10,000, but remember to break off the top left-hand corner before use), which can be bought at a tobacconist's or any shop displaying the white 'T' on a black background.

It is cheapest to call at off-peak times – 10am-8pm Mon.-Sat. and all day Sunday. The area code for Rome is 06, and you must dial this even for local numbers within Rome itself. For the European operator dial 15. To dial abroad you need to dial 00 followed by the country code and the number you require. The international country codes are as follows: UK 44, USA and Canada 1, Australia 61 and New Zealand 64. The cheapest time to make international calls is after 11pm.

CHANGING MONEY

Banks are open Mon. to Fri., 8.30am-1.30pm and 2.45-3.45pm. You may have to wait a long time for counter service. If you want to change foreign notes, you can also use the electronic exchange machines 24 hrs a day. These are usually installed in the walls of banks, or in tourist areas, stations and airports. If you have no other option, you can change money at the hotel reception, though never at a very advantageous rate.

You'll find some places prefer Eurocheques, though American Express, Mastercard, Visa and Diners cards are usually accepted. Tipping is recommended in restaurants, cafés, taxis and hotels (usually 10% of the bill). You can also take traveller's cheques (preferably from a well-known bank and in small denominations). Also see page 8.

TOURS AND OTHER ACTIVITIES

If you are not fluent in Italian but would like to learn more about Rome and its history, why not try a guided tour in English? There are various tours for the English speaker. Here are a few suggestions:

ENJOY ROME (Via Varese, 30) ☎ 445 18 43 offers tours guided by native English speakers. The guides are university graduates involved in teaching or in the humanities. They offer a wide range of walking tours including 'Ancient Old Rome', 'Vatican City Tour', 'Night Tour of Rome', and 'Jewish Rome and Trastevere'. For the more intrepid they also offer a fun 'Bike Tour'. The tours depart daily, come rain or shine, and cost L25000 for those under 26, and L30,000 for all others. Call for timetables, or visit: www.enjoyrome.com. This website also offers interesting links to other activities on offer in

Rome as well as maps, and information on hotels and restaurants.

In any case, you may also want to buy *Roma C'e*, available from kiosks. It's similar to *Time Out* magazine and includes full cinema, theatre and concert listings.

TOURIST OFFICES

The tourist office in Rome provides useful information and also arranges city tours. EPT, Via Parigi 5, ☎ 06 488 992 53. Note, tourist offices are recognisable by various acronyms: EPT, APT, AAST or IAT. It is a good idea to contact the Italian tourist office in your home country before you leave, in order to plan some of your weekend activities in advance and make the most of your time when you are in Rome. Italian tourist offices worldwide:

UK
1 Princes St, London W1R 9AY
☎ 020 7404 1254
(enitlond@globalnet.co.uk)

USA
630 Fifth Ave, suite 1565, New York, NY 10111
☎ 212 245 4822
(enitnv@bway.net)

or: 12400 Wilshire Blvd, Suite 550, Los Angeles, CA 90025
☎ 310 822 0098
or: 500 North Michigan Ave, Suite 2240, Chicago, IL 60611
☎ 312 644 0990

Canada
1 Place Ville Marie, Suite 1914, Montreal, Quebec H3B 2C3
☎ 514 866 7667
(739145@icam.net)

Australia
Alitalia, Orient Overseas Building, Suite 202, 32 Bridge St, Sydney 2000
☎ 02 9247 1308.

OPENING HOURS

The dates of the major public holidays are 21 April, 1 May, 2 June, 15 August, 1 November, and 8 and 26 December. Nowadays, shops which in the past used to be closed on Sundays, are increasingly open, though opening hours can vary. However, you won't find a street market for food on Sundays.

Lunchtime usually starts at 1-1.30pm, and dinner at 9-9.30pm. Public gardens are open from 7 or 9am-5pm. Many museums are closed in the afternoon and on Mondays. Most charge for admission. Children below the age of 12 are admitted free, though students are not eligible for reductions. Churches are open 7am-1pm and 4.30pm-7pm, to all who are appropriately dressed.

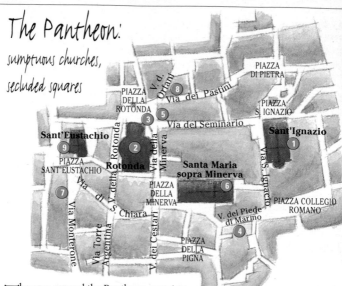

The Pantheon:
sumptuous churches,
secluded squares

The area around the Pantheon contains numerous piazzas and churches, but it is the Pantheon itself which dominates the surrounding streets with its huge dome. However, the sheer scale and beauty of this building can really only be appreciated from the inside. Despite such strong competition, the other churches nevertheless hold their own in terms of decoration. So if, after this extensive feasting of the eyes, you are in need of a little refreshment, try one of the many cafés sprinkled about the piazzas.

❶ Church of Sant'Ignazio ★★★
Piazza Sant'Ignazio.
Open every day 6am-12.30pm, 4.30-7.15pm.

The spectacular trompe-l'oeil decoration inside this church and the sumptuousness of its marble provide one of the most striking examples of the Counter Reformation's desire to impress the population. The same striking theatricality can be seen in the layout of the surrounding streets and squares.

❷ The Pantheon ★★★
Piazza della Rotonda.
Open every day 9am-6pm (5pm Oct. to Mar., Sun. 9am-1pm).

The Romans called the Pantheon, La Rotonda ('the round building'), because of its shape. It was built in AD 125 during the reign of the Emperor Hadrian and its originality lies in the giant central opening in its ceiling. The immensity of its circular interior, combined with the vast cupola or dome and the effects of light and shadow make this one of the most awe-inspiring sights in Rome.

❸ Replay ★
Piazza della Rotonda, 3.

If you like contrasts, and even if you're not interested in buying anything, nip into this

American clothes shop. With its typical 1950s American decor, complete with jukebox, motorbike and papier-maché figures, it would make an excellent set for an episode of 'Happy Days'.

❹ Le Pie' di Marmo ★★★
Via di Santo Stefano del Cacco.

It's not every day you turn a corner to come across a giant marble foot, in a street of the same name. This one once belonged to a Roman statue that probably decorated a temple. Popular belief in

the Middle Ages held that about half the population of Ancient Rome was made up of statues!

❺ Mail Art ★
Piazza della Rotonda.

This specialist shop is a real institution in the world of postcards. Here you'll find postcards in black and white recalling a distant and not-so-distant past, displayed in large albums which you're invited to leaf through. There are also colour postcards, useful for viewing some of the works in the museums you may not have time to visit. A very wide selection to choose from.

❻ Church of Santa Maria sopra Minerva ★★★
Piazza della Minerva, 42.
Open every day 7am-2pm, 4-7pm.

This church contains frescoes by Filippino Lippi and a beautiful sculpture of Christ by Michelangelo. The painter

Fra Angelico lies buried in one of the side chapels. The plain façade makes it difficult to guess at the riches inside. Make sure you also see the obelisk in front of the church supported on a small sculpted elephant by Bernini.

❼ L'EAU VIVE ★★
Via Monterone, 85
☎ 68 80 10 95.
Closed Sun.

A venue with a difference, housed in what was once a 16th century convent. Run by an order of nuns, the clientele ranges from the higher ranks of the international clergy to foreign politicians. The cuisine is French but all the dishes have Biblical names and refer to such events as the miracle of the loaves and fishes.

The Tazza d'Oro and Sant'Eustachio cafés ★★★
Via degli Orfani, 82
and piazza Sant'Eustachio.

Try to call in at the Tazza d'Oro ('the golden cup') ❽ and order their unique *granita di caffé* made with iced coffee and whipped cream, and perhaps buy some of the house coffee sold in hessian bags. The Sant'Eustachio café ❾ has an excellent reputation. Try their well-known *cappuccino*, as you rub shoulders with senators and members of parliament.

Piazza Navona: the show goes on

This fabulous Baroque piazza was given the perfect finishing touches by Bernini in the 17th century with his superb Fontana dei Fiumi (Fountain of the Four Rivers) and the sweeping façade of the church of Sant'Agnese in Agone on its western side, designed by Borromini. Today the piazza is full of life, people congregating around its three fountains to pass the time of day and catch some refreshing spray.

Map labels:
Via Zanardelli
Via dei Soldati
Via della Scrofa
PIAZZA DI TOR SANGUIGNA
V. S. Agostino
PIAZZA 5 LUNE
V. S. Giovanna d'Arco
S. Luigi d. Francesi
Santa Maria della Pace
PIAZZA
PIAZZA S. LUIGI DEI FRANCESI
Via Santa Maria dell'Anima
Corso del Rinascimento
Via di Salvatore FRANCESI
Palazzo Madama
Fontana d. Fiumi
NAVONA
V. Staderari
Sant' Ivo
Corso del Rinascimento
PIAZZA PASQUINO

❶ Piazza Navona ★★★

This most famous of Roman piazzas has retained the elongated form of the ancient Domitian stadium where all the most important public celebrations were held. Up until the middle of the 19th century, the piazza was flooded (by blocking the drains in the fountains) in August to refresh the people during the heat of summer. Nowadays, in December, Piazza Navona is covered in stalls selling products relating to the two high points of the winter – ornamental figures for Christmas, and toys for January 6 – the so-called 'day of the *Befana*', a fearsome witch who either brings children toys, if they've been good, or lumps of coal, if they've misbehaved.

❷ Café Tre Scalini ★★★
Piazza Navona.

All Romans come here for the house speciality, tartufo, an ice cream made with dark chocolate, or for the *granita di caffé*,

coffee poured over crushed ice (ideal on hot summer afternoons). And on the *terrasse*, portrait painters and fortune-tellers will do their best to help you pass the time.

❸ Fontana dei Fiumi
★★★

This fountain by Bernini (1651) testifies to one of history's greatest artistic rivalries. The statue, representing the Rio de la Plata river, is raising its arm as if to protect itself from the imminent collapse of the church of Sant'Agnese by Borromini, Bernini's great rival. Alongside it, the face of the statue representing the Nile is veiled so that it can't even see the façade of Borromini's work.

❹ Monasteri, Cinque Lune ★
**Piazza delle 5 Lune, 76
Corso Rinascimento, 89**

From inside their austere shop on Corso Rinascimento,

monks offer you the products of their labour – honey, biscuits, liqueurs, sweets and various other delicacies. Opposite is *Cinque Lune* ('the five moons'), the best patisserie in Rome – the kind of competition to delight those with a sweet tooth!

❺ Church of San Luigi dei Francesi
★★★
**Via Santa Giovanna d'Arco
Open every day 8am-12.30pm, 3.30-7pm.**

Go straight to the Contarelli chapel (at the back, to the right) where the three Caravaggio paintings are hung. The audacity of the paintings lies in their

❻ A STYLISH CAFÉ
★★★

The decor of Caffè della Pace, on the corner of Piazza Santa Maria della Pace, is reminiscent of certain rarefied, intimate 19th century interiors. From there, you can admire the portico of the church of Santa Maria della Pace, whose curves and counter-curves by Piero de Cortone make it one of the 16th century's most original façades. The good news for night-owls is that the café closes very late.

merciless realism and strong contrasted light. Such dramatic use of light made this painter of genius one of the darkest exponents of Baroque art.

❼ The Mario Praz collection ★★
**Palazzo Premoli,
Via Zanardelli
Tue.-Sun. 9am-6.30pm.**

As any interior decoration enthusiast will know, Mario Praz was an eccentric and erudite aesthete. His collection contains 1,057 items (paintings, wax miniatures, knick-knacks, toys, prints and more) mainly from the 19th century, all on display in his old apartment. It's a charming and unusual place, and not to be missed.

The historic city centre

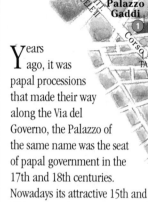

 Years ago, it was papal processions that made their way along the Via del Governo, the Palazzo of the same name was the seat of papal government in the 17th and 18th centuries. Nowadays its attractive 15th and 16th century houses remain, and this working class area is seeing new arrivals – fashionable restaurants (Baffetto, by far the best pizzeria in Rome), wine bars and various trendy shops (L'Una e l'altra, Arsenale), all of which are revitalising the area.

❶ Palazzo Gaddi
★★★
Via del Banco di Santo Spirito

Enter at no. 42 and admire the courtyard of Palazzo Gaddi, former residence of the wealthy banker, Chigi, who commissioned the best artists of the 16th century for its decoration. At no. 43, a bakery makes a crisp thin-crust pizza

that is taken out of the oven at exactly 11am every day. An appointment not to be missed!

❷ Piazza dell'Orologio ★★★

After undergoing lengthy restoration, Borromini's Clock Tower (17th century) is at last resplendent. Once again it

sports the iron bell support, from which ring out the hours regulating the daily life of the convent next door dedicated to the order of the Filippini. A mosaic of the Madonna adorns the side facing the street.

❸ Palazzo Taverna ★
Via Monte Giordano, 1
7am-8pm.

Don't be daunted by the imposing façade of this austere building, which is built on the ruins of a fortress once belonging to the Orsini. In the courtyard there is a massive fountain where you can enjoy the sight of water playing delicately against a dark green background of cypresses. Follow the somewhat labyrinthine layout of the building, which houses antique dealers, cabinet-makers and wrought iron craftsmen.

❹ Ditta Nani ★
Piazza Pasquino, 4

Opposite the famous Pasquino 'talking statue', on which people used to hang satiric poems written against the papal government, is a cloth and fabric shop dating back to 1874. It hasn't changed much since then and you'll find a profusion of fabrics filling the gloom under a vaulted ceiling amidst columns worthy of an ancient temple. It's worth seeing it for yourselves.

❺ Via dei Coronari ★★

This is the street of bric-a-brac and antique dealers. On weekends in May, they stay open until late. Many of the craftsmen repair furniture and other valuable items and can produce beautiful copies of old artworks. Behind the Palazzo Lancellotti, which has kept its shutters closed in protest at the reduction of papal authority over secular life, is *Il Telaio*, which mends and sells household linen.

❻ PRIMI DELLA CLASSE ★
Via del Governo Vecchio, 86
☎ 06 687 25 29

Signora Lo Conte should be given a medal for her pasta restaurant: for 37 years, the age of her son Alfonso, she has been making homemade pasta, and changes ingredients as often as she changes clothes. She delights in experimenting with different types of flour, running the results of the milling through her fingers to select the best one for the pasta she has in mind.

❼ In Folio ★
Corso Vittorio Emanuele II, 261

This is the perfect place to find design gifts: plates by Fornassetti decorated with enigmatic female faces, a toothbrush made from wild boar hair by Acca-Kappa, the parmesan knife designed by Aldo Rossi, stain-proof ties, and *Aurora 88*, the pen invented in 1947 by Nizzoli (very popular as a first communion gift for many Italians). It's a good place to buy unusual presents to take home.

Ditta Nani fabric shop.

Renaissance palaces and Campo dei Fiori

T he statue of Giordano Bruno, burnt alive in 1600 for heresy, is a reminder that Campo dei Fiori was once the site of public executions. Magnificent Renaissance palazzi still embellish the surroundings (still frequented by the Roman underworld), but nowadays the area is most famous for its bustling all-day market, restaurants and cheap clothes shops. One of the best places in central Rome to see authentic and typical daily life.

here would make a tasty little present to take back with you. These delicious titbits can also be eaten inside a piece of pizza *bianca* (plain, crisp and salted) bought from the next-door *Forno* (bakery) at no. 15. The pizza *rossa* (with tomatoes) is ideal for a light lunch, and their bread is legendary.

❶ Antica Norcineria ★★★
Viola, Piazza Campo dei Fiori, 43

The mini-sausages stuffed with fennel and the mountain *salame* from Tolfa on sale

❷ Palazzo Farnese ★★★
Piazza Farnese

After the death of the architect Sangallo in 1546, work on the unfinished building commissioned by Cardinal

Alessandro Farnese was taken over by Michelangelo, who added the imposing cornice. Find an excuse to go inside (it is now the French Embassy) and look at the courtyard, which has examples of the three Classical orders of columns, like the Colosseum.

The two tub-shaped fountains in the square outside were carved from the same granite block, and were originally brought back from Egypt in ancient times to decorate the Baths of Caracalla.

All kinds of trade

The Eastern tradition of having all craftsmen of the same profession housed in a single street known by the name of their trade dates back to the Middle Ages in Europe, and names such as Via dei Baullari (trunk makers), dei Cappellari (hat makers) and dei Chiavari (key makers), are an indication of the commercial importance this area once had. Nowadays you'll find clothes for young people at unbeatable prices.

❸ PALAZZO SPADA ★★★
Piazza Capo di Ferro, 13

Make sure you go and have a look at the superb trompe-l'oeil colonnade in the courtyard of Palazzo Spada (1540). Though only 9m/10yds long, it appears to be 37m/40yds long! Another detail to notice is the statue at the end of the colonnade that seems enormous and is in fact only 80cm/2ft 8in high.

❹ Teatro di Pompeo
Largo del Pallaro

The inauguration of this luxurious building witnessed the slaughter of 500 lions and 18 elephants. Today its only visible remains are in the dining room of the Costanza restaurant: follow the dark, narrow passageway leading from Piazza Grottapinta towards Piazza del Biscione. The passageway's gentle curve is that of the old theatre wall; it will lead you straight back to the time of Pompeii.

❺ Jam ★
Via dei Chiavari, 4
☎ 06 68 83 23 78

Don't be put off by the name of this relatively new restaurant and bar trading in splendid Renaissance surroundings on the site of

a Roman villa, the remains of which can be seen in the floor. Dishes include nettle risotto, salmon with provolone cheese, *millefeuilles* with gorgonzola, and ravioli stuffed with goat's cheese, all for your enjoyment.

❻ Spazio Sette ★★
Via dei Barbieri, 7
Open in August

This unusual shop is hardly noticeable from the street, as it is housed beyond the jungle of wisteria that is the courtyard, inside a Baroque building with a ceiling painted by the Giminiani brothers. It sells attractive design objects and modern furniture, and the ceramics and kitchen utensils would make original presents to take back home.

The medieval Ghetto

Rome has had a Jewish community for more than 2,000 years. It was forced to live in this area from 1555 following a decree by Pope Paul IV, but in 1848, the ghetto was abolished and its still principally Jewish inhabitants were released from the obligation to attend mass in neighbouring

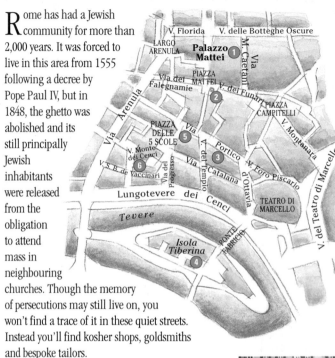

churches. Though the memory of persecutions may still live on, you won't find a trace of it in these quiet streets. Instead you'll find kosher shops, goldsmiths and bespoke tailors.

❶ Palazzo Mattei ★★

Via Caetani, 32. 7am-8pm

Palazzo Mattei is not far from the spot where the body of

Aldo Moro (executed by the 'Red Brigade') was discovered. Inside the courtyard is an amazing collection of ancient busts, statues, and friezes, which the architect, Maderno (1618), incorporated into a single Baroque decor, still bound to surprise any unsuspecting visitor.

❷ The Turtle Fountain ★★★
Piazza Mattei.

The pretty turtle fountain was designed by Giacomo della Porta and built by the goldsmith Taddeo Landini. It was restored in 1658 by

Bernini, who added the four turtles - the main reason the sculpture is now famous. The elegant design has been worn smooth over the years by the effects of the water, a key architectural element in the

17th century. Indeed, Baroque artists paid close attention to the sound water made, whether a gentle lapping, a murmur or a crashing cascade. But in this case, it was not the sound of the water arriving that counted, rather the music of the overflowing basin. Tucked away at the back of its courtyard, this fountain is one of the most secret and charming in Rome.

❸ Via Portico d'Ottavia

This is one of Rome's most picturesque streets, owing its

charm to the remains of the 300 columns of the Portico of Octavia (146 BC) that once enclosed temples dedicated to Jupiter and Juno. The Portico itself was erected by Augustus in honour of his sister, Octavia (23 BC). In the Middle Ages, the small church Sant'Angelo in Pescheria was built in the ruins not far from a large fish market. Nowadays, the area attracts old ladies who come to look out for and feed the numerous stray cats who live here.

❹ Isola Tiberina ★★

The whole island is occupied by the hospital of the Fatebenefratelli. Originally dedicated to the god of healing and protector against

the plague, Aesculapius, the island continues in its vocation today. During the great plague of 1656, all the sick were brought here in order to prevent the spread of disease, and the island has always had few inhabitants. It's a useful shortcut to get from the Ghetto to Trastevere. You just need to cross the bridge, built by the consul Fabricius in 62 BC and which still bears his name.

❺ Limentani ★
Via Portico d'Ottavia, 47

The only clue to the family business inside is a marble

plaque outside, etched with the name Limentani. This family has always sold household articles from this enormous, darkened basement. You'll find fine porcelain and inexpensive crystal glasses, as well as cutlery and a large selection of kitchen utensils.

❻ PIPERNO ★★★
Via Monte dei Cenci, 9
☎ 06 68 80 27 72.
Closed Sun. eve.

This well-known restaurant serves Jewish-Roman cuisine, including *carciofi alla giudia*, delicious fried peppered artichokes with tender hearts. In summer, meals are served on the terrace, and in winter, inside the dining room with frescoed walls. Eating here can be expensive, but Piperno does have one of the best wine lists in Rome.

The Vatican City and surroundings

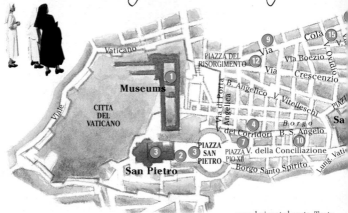

The papal residence was built over the tomb of St Peter and is really a city within a city, or rather, since 1929, a state within a city. It comprises a huge basilica, 11 museums, the restored Sistine chapel, the Swiss Guard, a radio station broadcasting all over the world, a television station, a daily newspaper, all signposted, in a highly-sophisticated system of organisation. More than a thousand residents are responsible for the smooth, day-to-day running of this nerve centre of official Christianity, with of course the Pope at its head. Here are some pointers:

❶ The Vatican Museums ★★★

Entrance in Viale Vaticano. Mon.-Sat. and last Sun. of month 8.45am-1pm, Mon.-Fri. Jul.-Sep. and Easter 8.45am-4pm. Closed on public and religious holidays.
Entrance charge. There is a bus service from the museums to St Peter's Square.

This is one of the world's greatest collections of Classical and Renaissance art, as well as Greek and Roman antiquities. Visitors are expected to follow the one-way designated route. Try to save some astonishment for the Raphael rooms and the Sistine chapel at the end.

❷ The Swiss Guard ★

The papal guard of hired Swiss soldiers was created in 1505 and may owe its uniform to Michelangelo. It's one that's difficult to miss – baggy trousers, tight wasp-waisted jerkin with wide sleeves, all in midnight-blue and duck-yellow stripes, with the red of the underclothing showing - not to mention the white gloves and ruffle, feathered iron helmet, halberd, and sword! The Guard is made

Baroque canopy in the nave of St Peter's and the canons of the Castel San Angelo made of bronze taken from the vault of the Pantheon. Small souvenir bells are on sale here.

❺ Ruschena ★★
Lungotevere dei Mellini, 1
☎ **06 320 44 49**

Whilst you're under papal protection, why not commit the sin of greed by trying a *millefeuille* in this patisserie that also serves meals. It's an old-fashioned, almost dusty, place of great charm, popular as much with elderly ladies as with young people. It also has a good view over the Tiber and the domes of Rome.

❻ Castel Sant' Angelo ★★★
Apr.-Sep., 9am-6pm, Oct.-Mar., 9am-2pm (last admission 1hr before closing time) Closed on public holidays.

❼ Papal Blessings ★
Galerie Savelli, Piazza Pie XII, 2.

If your cousin is getting married or you're invited to the baptism of your best friend's new baby, why not buy a papal blessing (L35,000-50,000) dated and signed by the Apostolic Archbishop Chaplain, i.e. the Pope himself, who will do his best for the recipient.

This fortress was first built as a mausoleum for the Emperor Hadrian (AD130-139), but it has also been a prison and a papal residence. The museum inside retraces its history. It also has a corridor linking it with the Vatican. As in the last act of *Tosca*, admire the beautiful view from the terrace but don't throw yourself off – go for a coffee instead in one of the rampart towers.

up of four officers, 23 NCOs, 70 halberdiers and 2 drummers, all of whose job it is to watch over the sacred figure of the *Pontif*.

❸ St Peter's Basilica and Square ★★★
Basilica, 7am-7pm (6pm Oct.-Mar.) Admission charge for the Cupola and Treasury.

Both form part of a vast, magnificent whole. The main courtyard has a spectacular curving colonnade by Bernini and 140 statues of saints surmount the upper balustrade. The basilica is a testimony to the forms and history of Roman art. A good time to visit is during the papal benediction (midday, Sun).

❹ Fonderia Luccichenti (the Vatican foundry) ★★
Vicolo del Farinone (Piazza Città Leonina)

The open-roofed Vatican foundry has existed since the 16th century. It was here that were built, amongst other things, the extraordinary

vendors sell pure silk imitation designer ties at excellent prices. Museums and shopping – the perfect combination for an enjoyable day in the city.

⓫ Eredi Pisano ★
Via Cola di Rienzo, 214-218

The split levels give this vast shop an undeniably intimate atmosphere. This is where you'll find all the basics of Roman fashion, for both men and women. The clothes are simply cut, sporty designs, and you'll be able to buy your whole wardrobe – coats, suits, shirts, ties and headscarves, shoes, and even underwear.

⓬ L'Altra Moda ★
Via Cola di Rienzo, 54

This shop, which is part of a well-established chain of nine others in Rome, is very popular with Roman women. They love its copies of classic designer styles, such as Max Mara or Armani. You'll find colourful clothes for all ages, with well-cut ladies' suits at very attractive bargain prices.

⓭ Roxy ties
Via Cola di Rienzo, 313

Despite the English name, the style is Italian. The ties are displayed in glass showcases like some vast 19th-century insect collection (around L30,000).

❽ Enoteca Constantini
Piazza Cavour, 16

The basement of this wine shop decorated in Art

Nouveau style houses vast cellars of wines. You'll receive good advice and information and soon know all you need to about Chianti and Barolo,

before going upstairs to try some for yourself (though tasting is only possible in the evenings) with *crostini*.

❾ Via Cola di Rienzo

This is the biggest shopping street near the Vatican. A perfect way to spend a day would be to visit the museums in the morning and come here after lunch to shop for good quality, reasonably priced clothes. You'll find all kinds of interesting and unusual items on sale that you simply can't buy in England, especially men's clothes. And the street

also find yourselves tempted to buy some of their chocolates or olive oil to take back home with you. Franchi is an example of the best that catering in Rome has to offer. You can even enjoy some of it on the spot.

⑯ Barilla ★
Corner of Via Cola di Rienzo and Via Tacito

This luxury shoe company has opened a shop for a younger generation of clients

⑭ Eredi
Via Cola di Rienzo, 127

Eredi means heirs. In this case, if the decor of this elegant lingerie shop is anything to go by (sculpted cherry wood with painted floral motifs), heirs to a 1920s style. The basement is reserved for special offers. This is excellent-quality lingerie certain to create a sensation. Afterwards, why not drop in for an ice cream at Pellacchia at no. 103?

⑮ Castroni et Franchi ★
Via Cola di Rienzo, 196

This part of the street is a gourmet's paradise: Castroni make excellent coffee (which you don't have to drink on the premises). You may well

who don't want to be penniless fashion victims. You'll still find all the classic styles, but they are constantly reinvented and updated to take account of the latest trends. But Barilla is also the master of classic and timeless Italian shoe designs – white moccasins for men, pastel ones for women.

❿ THE OLD BORGO DISTRICT ★★

Situated between the Tiber, the Vatican, Via Cola di Rienzo and Via della Conciliazione, is the old Borgo district. As soon as the first St Peter's basilica had been built, other chapels sprang up around it. The Pope naturally decided to enclose and fortify the

area in order to ensure the protection of these various sanctuaries, considered part of the Vatican. Nevertheless, after the fall of Rome, the Borgo was abandoned by its noble residents, and the area soon became one of the poorest in the city. The whole district was entirely redesigned in the 20th century and replaced by wide streets intersecting at right angles, effacing all traces of the old 'village'. So whilst Via della Conciliazione, built during the 1920s, opened up a perspective onto St Peter's, it also wiped away one of Rome's most picturesque locations.

Piazza del Popolo

In the past, the painters of the Roman school had their studios in Via Margutta. Some even attended the 'artists' mass' celebrated in the church of Santa Maria del Popolo. Nowadays the piazza and its surroundings are a busy commercial area with attractive inexpensive shops.

Santa Maria del Popolo ②

PIAZZA DEL POPOLO ①

Tridente ③

④ ⑦

Via de Vantaggio   V. Laurina   Via Margutta   V. d. Fontanella

Via Gesù e Maria del   V. S. Giacomo   Babuino

Via Canova   Via dei Greci

Via della Frezza   Via Vittoria dell'Oca

Via Ara Pacis   Via Belsiana

⑤ **Ara Pacis Augustæ**

PIAZZA AUGUSTO IMPERATORE   Corso

Via Tomacelli ⑧   LARGO GOLDONI ⑥

Ripetta

❶ Piazza del Popolo ★★★

The monumental Renaissance gateway based on the style of the ancient Roman triumphal arches was started in 1565 and completed by Bernini a century later. It forms a grandiose entrance to the piazza and underwent successive elaborate changes, resulting, at the beginning of the 19th century, in the elegant neo-classical style we see today.

❷ Church of Santa Maria del Popolo ★★★
**Piazza del Popolo, 12
Open every day 7am-noon, 4-7pm**

The plain exterior and façade provide no clues to the masterpieces hidden inside. The interior was worked on by some of the greatest artists of the 15th to 17th century – Raphael, Pinturicchio, Sebastiano del Piombo, Salviati and Caravaggio (don't miss his *Crucifixion of Saint Peter*). The church was financed by donations from the local working population (hence the name, which means '...of the people'), who wanted to erase the ghost of Nero, once said to haunt the site.

❸ The Tridente
★★★

The *Tridente* is the popular name given to the three very different streets that lead onto Piazza del Popolo – Via del Babuino, Via del Corso and Via Ripetta. The first is more upmarket and mostly lined with antique dealers, the second, once famous for the horse races that took place along its 1.5km/1 mile length, is now an inexpensive shopping street, and the third is where artists come to buy their materials and paints.

❹ Macelleria Mastrodi ★
Via di Ripetta, 236

This butcher's is one of the most beautiful shops decorated in the Art Nouveau style. The marble, bronze and precious wood decor is unique, and

features a counter not dissimilar to a village church pulpit lit from above by a lamp in the form of a winged dragon. It all started in 1893, when a butcher with avant-garde tastes decided he wanted to make his shop more inviting as he cut the meat in front of his customers. Do go inside and have a look, even if you're vegetarian.

❺ Ara Pacis Augustae ★★★
Via di Ripetta
Mon.-Sat. 9am-7pm, Sun. 9am-1pm. Admission charge.

This altar commemorates the peace created by the Emperor Augustus after his

victorious campaigns in Gaul and Spain (13-9 BC). Since 1937, a feat of archaeological ingenuity has allowed the monument to be pieced together from the various fragments that had spread throughout the world. It's a fine example of Roman art at the time of the Empire.

❻ Merola ★★
Via del Corso, 143

This glove shop was opened by the Merola brothers in 1920 and still has the original furnishings. The elegant panelling and 125 drawers hark back to an era when high society ladies would meet for

fittings 'chez Merola'. The walls are decorated with certificates and medals.

❼ Edy ★
Vicolo del Babuino, 4
☎ 06 36 00 17 38
Open until 2am.

Tagliatelle as delicately thin as the hair of an angel, airy ravioli, skilful blendings of vegetables – such authentic cooking is somewhat of a rarity in this essentially tourist area.

❽ LA BANCA DEL FUCINO ★

Via Tomacelli, 106
Mon.-Fri. 8.30am-1pm, 3-4.30pm.

Even if you don't have any deposits to make, you should drop by this bank that once belonged to Prince Torlonia. The interior is a wonderful example of Viennese Art Nouveau, with a profusion of marble, sculpted wood and furniture. Of note, too, are the large tables lit by a central lamp and the stuccoed ceiling.

Luxury and glamour around Piazza di Spagna

Poussin, Claude Lorrain and other French artists all lived in this area in the 17th century and were among the first to bring it to the attention of others.

In the 18th century, it became very cosmopolitan and this is still true today. This is where you'll find the most exclusive fashions and designers, in the luxury boutiques of the narrow streets radiating from Piazza di Spagna.

the start of the 18th century. It's not unusual to come across famous people followed by their *scorta* (bodyguard) or a *paparazzo*. This is one of the liveliest and most colourful places in Rome, so sit down and spend a while watching life go by. Down in the middle of the square is the Barcaccia fountain (1627), which resembles a sinking boat.

displays attract crowds of onlookers, tourists, some wealthy customers and the occasional pickpocket. And in surroundings as charming as Via Condotti, it's not unknown to meet an Italian playboy or two.

❶ Piazza di Spagna ★★★

Accentuated by the restricted proportions of the piazza, the effect of the broad stairway rising up to the Church of Trinité dei Monti is splendidly theatrical. The landings and flowing ramps were built at

❷ Via Condotti ★★★

It is from this pedestrian street that some of the most renowned fashion houses – Bulgari, Gucci, Prada, Biagiotti, La Perla, Ferragamo – sell their latest creations. Their exquisite window

❸ Babington's Tea Rooms ★★
Piazza di Spagna, 23
9am-8pm, closed Sun.

Founded in 1896, these elegant tea rooms have a very 'British' atmosphere, not without a hint of snobbery. Nevertheless, there's still

There are also stalls selling prints, magazines and old books of a much better quality than those on offer at the very touristy market near the station.

enough intimacy amidst the sober furniture, patisserie displays and polished wooden floor to help you feel relaxed and a little at home.

❻ Rioda ★★
Via Belsiana, 90
☎ 06 678 44 35

It's worth finding your way up the narrow stairs to this leather goods shop on the first floor, opened by

❹ Palazzo Borghese ★★
Largo Fontanella Borghese
7am-10pm.

The building itself isn't very appealing. It was built in the early 17th century and somewhat resembles a prison. The courtyard, open to the public, is much more attractive as it has a nymphaeum with three fountains known as the 'Bath of Venus', built by Rainaldi in 1665. Have a look too at the banister and the superb oval lift cabin in precious wood. The painting collection once housed here is now in the museum of the Villa Borghese.

❺ The print market ★★
Largo Fontanella Borghese
7am-1pm. Closed Sun.

Browse around under the large square parasols. You may get lucky and find a reasonably-priced 18th century engraving by Piranesi.

a family of craftsmen and women. Very much the old style of retailer, the quality of the work is excellent and in the dim recesses of their

apartment, you'll find handbags based on the more popular designs by Gucci and Hermès and selling at a fraction of the price.

❼ THE BRION VEGA RADIO AT ORAZI ★★★
Largo Fontanella Borghese, 89
☎ 06 68 87 34 02

The TS 502 radio, designed in 1964 by Zanuso, is a delight. It resembles a black cube, but only reveals its true purpose when pulled open. It's one of Italy's best design inventions. A surprisingly inexpensive item that makes a great gift.

Memories of 'La Dolce Vita' on Via Veneto

When, in 1886, Rome's town planners decided to build a street linking Piazza Barberini with Villa Borghese, it meant razing the grounds of the Ludovisi residence even though they were considered 'the world's most beautiful garden'. Sadly, the resulting road, the Via Veneto, today no longer even has the prestige it enjoyed in the 1930s and 1950s, but is instead asphyxiated by heavy traffic and fumes.

❶ Doney ★
Via Veneto, 145

This café, started in the 1940s by a family of English pastry-cooks, owes its renown to Fellini's film *La Dolce Vita*. Doney used to be the place where the stars of the big screen would gather on a warm summer evening, often under the intrusive flashlights of the paparazzi. Today,

you're more likely to meet Japanese tourists.

❷ The Majestic Hotel ★
Via Veneto, 50

This luxury hotel was renamed Maestoso by Mussolini, who banned foreign names. It still has its original lounges and to the Italians, the bar has a very 'British' atmosphere, with its hushed calm and plush armchairs. The ideal place to stop for a break and sip a Campari in peace.

❸ Albanese ★
Via Lazio, 14

This shoe shop's regular clientele includes Cinderellas such as Elizabeth Taylor and Kim Basinger. The business is now run by the son, Vicenzo, who is a fan of the 1950s style. Unfortunately, the prices have kept up with inflation - not that certain Cinderellas would notice.

❹ Palombi ★★★
Via Veneto, 114.

The pasta here comes in all shapes and colours. It'll be hard to choose from such a wide selection of often original recipes – made with radish, mushrooms, eggs, fennel, and avocado. Fresh pasta really is the tastiest and so it's worth remembering that it

will easily keep for two weeks if left unwrapped and in the open. Ensure it's not wrapped in plastic.

❺ Piazza Barberini ★★

Piazza Barberini is the site of two statues by Bernini. One is small and to be found on the corner of Via Veneto, apparently providing the bees of the Barberini coat of arms with water to drink. The other, standing in the centre of the piazza, is of an immense Triton. At the time, its realism was considered very avant-garde.

❻ Palazzo Barberini ★★★
Via delle Quattro Fontane, 13.
Tue.-Sat. 9am-2pm, Sun. 9am-1pm.
Admission charge.

This building was the combined work of Borromini and Bernini (1633). It houses the Museum of Ancient Art, with its important collection of paintings from the 13th to 16th centuries. Don't miss the trompe-l'oeil The *Triumph of Providence* by Piero da Cortona which decorates the vaulted ceiling of the central salon. It is quite stunning.

❽ THE RAPE OF SAINT THERESA ★★★
Via XX Settembre, 17
Every day 6.30am-noon, 4.30-6pm.

In the Cornaro chapel of the church of Santa Maria della Vittoria is one of Bernini's most audacious works (1646). The sensuality depicted in this famous sculpture has given rise to many works of interpretation, including a new approach to female sexuality by the French psychoanalyst Lacan (Séminaire XX) - definitely quite an undertaking!

❼ Church of Santa Maria della Concezione ★★★
Via Veneto, 27
Every day 9am-noon, 3-6pm.
Donations welcome.

The crypt in this church is both fascinating and sinister, since Capuchin monks have covered the walls of five chapels with the skulls of their dead brethren – about 4,000 of them. It's a far cry from the nonchalant luxury of the hotels, bars and boutiques of Via Veneto. A guaranteed shocker.

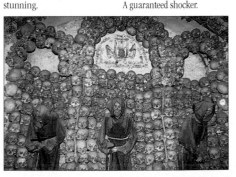

The Trevi Fountain: water from wine

Though many people remember the voluptuous Anita Ekberg taking a nocturnal bath in front of the statue of Neptune in Fellini's *La Dolce Vita*, not everyone will know that restoration work on the fountain was carried out thanks to the taxes collected on wine! But Rome is not just a Baroque backdrop to the antics of stars and *paparazzi*. The warren of narrow streets at the foot of the Quirinale presidential residence are a reminder that this is also where craftsmen and small traders continue to work and go about their daily business.

Map labels: P. D. FONTANA DI TREVI ①; V. d. Lavatore; V. d. Pannetteria; Palazzo del Quirinale ⑥; V. del Quirinale; Via del Quirinale ⑦; Piacenza; ③ V. d. Muratte; Via dell' Umiltà; V. d. Dataria; Salita Monte; PIAZZA DEL QUIRINALE; V. della Consulta; V. Parma; V. Nazionale; V. SS. Apostoli; V. d. Modesti; Vaccaro; V. d. Pilotta; ④ Mazzarino; ② V. SS. APOSTOLI; PIAZZA SS. APOSTOLI; Palazzo Colonna ⑤; V. IV Novembre; V. 24 Maggio; Via

① The Trevi Fountain ★★★

Its name derives from its position at the end of three streets ('*tre vie*'). By day (and, better still, by night) the 18th-century fountain by Nicolo Salvi depicting an aquatic Bacchanalian spectacle continues to astonish visitors. If you want to guarantee your return one day to the Eternal City, the custom is to throw a coin over your left shoulder into the water.

② Via Nazionale ★

At the start of the century, this was the most elegant street in Rome. Though it has lost some of its attraction it remains one of the city's busiest shopping streets, and has many affordable shoe shops popular with the young. The main attraction is the Palazzo delle Esposizioni (Rome main exhibition centre), which always has something interesting on.

③ Al Moro ★★
Vicolo delle Bollette, 13
☎ 06 678 34 95. Closed Sun. and August. Best to reserve.

This is a lively place, popular with politicians. The Roman cooking here is of good quality: excellent fried fish, a good selection of vegetables and delicious *baccalà* – dried cod.

It's here, in one of Rome's most sumptuous Baroque interiors, that you'll find the famous *The Beaneater* by Annibale Carracci, founder of the Bolognese school.

❻ Palazzo del Quirinale ★★★

This is where you will see Rome at its most theatrical — monumental stairways, gardens, turrets, palazzi,

❹ Moriondo and Gariglio ★★★

Via della Pilotta, 2.
Mon.-Sat. in winter, Mon.-Fri. in summer, 9am-1pm, 3.30-7.30pm.

Chocolate lovers should adore this establishment and its homemade chocolates, of which there are more than 50 types, including an extra-dark chocolate called 'poison'. And if chocolates are not your thing, then let yourself be tempted by the marrons glacés, the other house speciality.

❺ Palazzo Colonna art gallery ★

Via della Pilotta, 17
9am-1pm, Sat. (last admissions midday).
Closed in August.
Admission charge.

colossal statues, and even an Egyptian obelisk. This was once the summer residence of the popes. It then became the royal residence of the kings of Italy, and today it is the official residence of the President of the Republic. Once a year, on 12 June, he opens his doors to the public and allows his guests to drink the water from his private spring.

❼ CHURCH OF SANT'ANDREA AL QUIRINALE ★★★

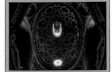

Via del Quirinale, 29
Wed.-Mon. 10am-noon, 4-7pm

Though Bernini considered this church (1658), with its elegant oval design and clever visual effects, to be some of his best work, he would not have been unaware of the nearby superb cupola crowning Borromini's masterpiece, the church of San Carlo alle Quattro Fontane (at no. 23 in the same street, open every day 9.30am-12.30pm, 4-6pm, Sun. only during mass).

The Roman Forum, an open-air museum

This superb collection of buildings and remains, one of the most famous in the world, was discovered when Napoleon ordered the excavation of this site, which had become little more than pastureland for cows. Nowadays, the 'lawyers, litigants, praetors, traders, shopkeepers, prostitutes and other good-for-nothings' from the time of writer Plautus (3rd to 2nd century BC) have been replaced by hordes of tourists, amateur archeologists and people out for a stroll. But these impressive remains of the ancient Roman republic are among the highlights of any stay.

❶ The Palatine Hill
★★★

Entrance in Via di San Gregorio, or through the Forum, 9am-2pm. Admission charge valid for both sites.

Augustus, Tiberius, Caligula, Domitian, Nero and Septimus Severus all had palaces on this hillside. Now the Palatine is a small poetic landscape of umbrella pines and lawns affording a splendid view over the domes and rooftops of the city. It's worth visiting the Flavian palace, and the House of Livia for its frescoes.

❷ The Forum ★★★
Entrance in Via dei Fori Imperiali, Mon.-Sat. 9am until 2hrs before nightfall, Sun. 9am-2pm.

A maze of evocative ruins crossed by the Via Sacra, which is pleasant to wander along. Perhaps of greatest interest are the Arch of Septimus Severus erected in 203, the eight columns of the Temple

to Saturn, the House of the Vestal Virgins with its vast atrium, the Portico of the Temple to Antonin and Faustina, which hides the Baroque façade of San Lorenzo in Miranda, and the Arch of Titus.

❸ The Basilica of Constantine and Maxentius ★★★

Three giant arches stand out along the Via Sacra and are part of an original building that must once have covered an area measuring 100m/109yds by 65m/71yds . Clearly its founder wanted to be remembered by the people who frequented the basilica. Housed in one of the apses was once a giant statue of Constantine.

❹ The Colosseum ★★★

9am-7pm, Oct.-Mar., 3pm, Sun. 9am-1pm. Closed on public holidays. Admission charge.

Work on Rome's largest amphitheatre was started in AD 72 during the reign of Vespasian and the last event was held in AD 523. As the name suggests, the Colosseum is colossal, and has a circumference of over 500m/550yds. As many as 60,000 spectators could delight in watching

gladiatorial combats, or the slaughter of wild animals and Christian martyrs.

❺ The Trajan Column ★★

This column measures over 40m/130ft and its shaft, made up

of 17 stacked marble drums, is a sculpted spiralling frieze depicting more than 2,500 figures. The scenes are drawn from the Emperor Trajan's victorious campaigns in Dacia (now Romania) and tell the full story from the departure from Rome to the retreat of the enemy.

❻ Trajan's Markets ★★★

Via IV Novembre, Thu. and Sat. 9am-1pm, Apr.- Sep. 9am-6pm, closed Mon. Admission charge.

UP ON HIGH

If you need to take a break, pause at the summit of the Palatine Hill in what was once was the Farnese garden ❼ – a delightful, peaceful place overlooking the ruins of the forum. If you're feeling peckish, try the roof terrace of the Forum Hotel (Via Tor de Conti, 25 ☎ 06 679 24 46) ❽ for lunch – you'll have the ruined capital of the ancient world lying at your feet.

This ancient market was made up of 150 shops, warehouses and taverns, located over three floors. People came here to buy everything from silk, fresh fish and vegetables to jewels, wine and cereals. Few women

ever came to this immense complex as shopping was considered men's work. Some things have certainly changed.

The Capitol: capital of the ancient world

The *Mirabilia Urbis Romae*, the oldest guide to the Capitol, describes this as *'caput mundi'* – the capital of the world. It was once the centre of religious life in the Roman republic, and standing on the very summit of the Capitoline Hill was the Temple to Jupiter. Today the Capitol is still considered the symbolic centre of Rome, and, as the seat of local government, continues to be where marriages and other ceremonies are held. The present arrangement dates back to the 17th century and was designed by Michelangelo.

❶ Piazza del Campidoglio ★★★

Standing on top of the Capitoline Hill, this piazza redesigned by Michelangelo in the mid 16th century, took some 100 years to complete. In the shape of a trapezium with geometrically patterned paving, it is flanked by the Palazzi dei Conservatori

and Nuovo which form the Capitoline museums. Two huge statues of the mythological twins, Castor and Pollux, gaze out from the top of the *cordonata* (staircase) leading up to the square.

❷ The Capitoline Museums ★★★

Piazza del Campidoglio 9am-7pm, Wed.-Sun. 9am-2pm. Admission charge (except 1st Sun. of month) also valid for Palazzo dei Conservatori.

Before entering the Palazzo Nuovo, the only museum in the

world dedicated to sculpture, go and see the giant hand and head from the statue of Constantine II in the courtyard of the Palazzo dei Conservatori (opposite). In one piece, the statue must have stood over 12m/38ft tall. Inside, the busts of Roman philosophers and emperors are sculpted with remorseless realism.

❸ The Cordonata ★★★

Climb towards heaven, or towards glory, when you go up one of these two very different staircases. The 122 steps leading up to the Aracoeli church represent a certain way of seeing life in the Middle Ages as one long, hard pilgrimage from earth to heaven. The Cordonata, on the other hand, is a gently-sloping ramp rising up to the Capitol in homage to the Emperor Charles V, who defeated the Muslim infidels.

❹ Statue of Marcus Aurelius ★★★
Piazza del Campidoglio

During the Middle Ages, the most famous equestrian bronze statue of the ancient world (2nd century) was saved from vandalism by a legend that warned of the end of the world should the statue regain its original golden hue. The original is now in the museum and an exact replica (created with the aid of computer technology) now stands in its place.

❺ Church of Santa Maria in Aracoeli ★★★

Piazza d'Aracoeli
Open every day 7am-noon, 4-6pm (Jun.-Sep. 6.30pm)

Erected over the ruins of a temple dedicated to a pagan goddess that later became a church dedicated to the cult of the Virgin Mary, this church is a fine example of how sacred sites changed from age to age. The 22 columns that separate the three naves and lead to the frescoes by Pinturicchio (16th century) were all taken from various ancient buildings.

❻ Vecchia Roma ★
Piazza Campitelli
☎ 06 686 46 04

The guidebook of *Espresso* magazine gives 15/20 and 2 'chef's hats' to this traditional restaurant located alongside the Baroque façade of the church of Santa Maria in Campitelli. Even if you're not going to dine there, walk round the piazza – in the evenings and you'll hear the murmur of the Della Porta fountain blend in with the cries of the seagulls up from the Tiber on the lookout for tasty morsels.

THE HOLY CHILD OF ARACOELI

This particular 'Holy Child' is a statue of the infant Jesus, sculpted in a piece of olive wood taken from the Garden of Gethsemane. The precious stones that once adorned it have been stolen, but its miraculous power is said to be unaffected. The statue has the power to cure the sick (whereupon its lips turn red!) and is regularly taken across Rome by taxi to the various hospitals where it is required.

The Aventine Hill: a haven of peace

The Aventine was one of the original seven hills of Rome and now houses an unassuming residential district overlooking the Tiber. It's a wonderful place to stroll, amidst gardens and shuttered villas, and the serene beauty of the palaeo-Christian churches. Since ancient times, it has been the dream of Romans to retire here. The name comes from Aventinus, a descendant of Aeneas who, it is said, was struck by lightning and buried where he died.

PIAZZA BOCCA DELLA VERITÀ

Av. della Greca

Clivio dei Publici

Clivo di Publici

Parco di S. Alessio

Tevere

Lungotevere

Aventino

Santa Sabina

Sant' Alessio

Via di Santa Sabina

PIAZZA DEI CAVALIERI DI MALTA

Via

V. Porta Lavernale

Marmorata

Via Pollione

❶ Bocca della Verita ★

Only the truth comes out of the mouth of a marble plaque in the form of a lion's head decorating the porch of the church of Santa Maria in Cosmedin (9am–7pm). A medieval legend has it that the 'mouth of truth' will bite the hand of any liar. Don't leave without noticing the skilful use of colours in the 18th-century flooring created by the famous Cosma brothers.

❷ The Orange Gardens ★
Via S. Sabina, 1
From dawn to dusk

Also known as the Parco Savello (the name of the nearby fortress built by the Savelli in the 13th century), this small garden planted with pine and orange trees, with alleys lined with potted laurels, is the setting for a theatre festival on summer evenings. From its superb terrace above the Tiber, there's a revealing view of Trastevere and the medieval Ghetto.

Church of Santa Maria in Cosmedin.

❸ Church of Santa Sabina ★★

Open every day 6am-12.45pm, 3.30-6pm

It was here in 1222 that Saint Dominic presented his order to Pope Honorious III. Since then the basilica, which was built in the 5th century and restored in the 13th century, has belonged to the Dominicans. Don't enter the nave without having seen the sculpted main door, one of the original panels of which (top right) is one of oldest depictions of the crucifixion.

❹ Piazza Cavalieri di Malta ★★★

The piazza, designed by Piranesi in about 1765, has

a slightly military appearance due to the high encircling walls. There's a surprise waiting for you at no. 3, put your eye up to the keyhole and you'll see the dome of St Peter's, solitary and shimmering in the light, framed at the end of one of the tree-lined alleyways of the priory. It's here too that on Sunday mornings you can hear the Gregorian chants in the church attached to the Benedictine seminary of Sant'Anselmo.

❺ Church of Santi Bonifacio e Alessio ★

Piazza di Sant'Alessio, 23 Open every day 8.30am-noon, 3.30-6.30pm (Oct.-Mar., 5pm)

To the left of the nave is a Baroque chapel housing an unusual relic. It is said to be part of the staircase under which the martyr Alessio died. Escaping an arranged marriage, Alessio fled his wealthy patrician family, returning some years later dressed in rags. No one recognised him and for 17 years he worked as a servant in his old family house, sleeping under the stairs and only revealing his true identity on his deathbed..

❻ Volpetti ★★★

Via Marmorata, 47 9am-2pm, 5-8pm

Volpetti is one of the best restaurants in town and a hallowed place for Roman cooking. Don't be embarrassed to ask for a *panino* (sandwich), which comes in thinly-sliced bread and charcuterie, or for one of the 180 types of cheese on offer. Romans also come here to buy delicious regional specialities and tinned truffles.

❼ THE ROSE GARDEN ★★

Clivio dei Pubblicii 9am-7pm

The best period to visit this small garden is May to June, when the 5,000 rose bushes are in full bloom and blending their delicate smells and colours. The splendid view over the Palatine ruins makes it even more romantic.

Country in the city: the Celian Hill

Via Labicana
Via di San
Via del SS.
Via Capo d'Africa
San Clemente ①
Giovanni in Laterano
Quattro Coronati ⑤
Santi Quattro Coronati
Via Celimontana
Via Claudia
Basilica of S. Giovanni e Paolo ⑥
Via di Santo Stefano Rotondo
Santo Stefano Rotondo ②
Via di S. Erasmo
Villa Celimontana
Via della Navicella
Via Amba
Aradam
Viale Manzoni
Via Merulana
Vi della Fontana
PIAZZA S. GIOVANNI IN LATERANO
San Giovanni in Laterano ③
④ ⑦

The Celian Hill, one of Rome's seven hills, is an unusual mix of small apartment blocks, barracks, gardens, churches and Roman remains, all located within the area between the Colosseum and Porta S. Giovanni. After being sacked by the Normans in 1084, the hill became increasingly uninhabited, remaining in a virtual natural state until the end of the 19th century which has lent it an agreeable country feel.

① Church of San Clemente ★★★
Via San Giovanni in Laterano
Open every day 9am–12.30pm, 3.30–6.30pm. Admission charge for the lower levels.

San Clemente offers a summary of Roman history on three levels, through three places of worship from three different eras. Be sure to see inside the church at street level (12th century) and the mosaics in the side chapel illustrating the crucifixion; also in the church on the

level below, the 11th-century frescoes (dating from the Carolingian and Roman periods) and, on the lowest level, the altar to Mithras.

② Church of Santo Stefano Rotondo ★★★
Via di Santo Stefano Rotondo, 7
9am–noon.

This circular 5th-century church may have been used as a Roman abattoir. In any case, it's an interesting example of the re-use of materials. The 16th-century frescoes form a kind of diorama depicting graphic

torture scenes that would have delighted the Marquis De Sade.

❸ Basilica of San Giovanni in Laterano ★★★

Piazza San Giovanni in Laterano, 4
Basilica open every day 7am-7pm (Oct.-Mar., 6pm), cloister 9am-5pm in winter and 9am-6pm in summer.

Rome's cathedral was the first Christian basilica to be built in the town under Constantine in AD 313 . All popes were crowned here until 1870. It has been burnt down twice, though the cloister (which, like the baptistery, is worth a visit) miraculously escaped any damage. The monumental façade that you see today was finished in 1735 by Alessandro Galilei and the interior by Borromini in 1646.

❹ Da Nerone
Via delle Terme di Tito, 96
☎ 06 47 45 207

This restaurant only a short distance form the Colosseum is popular with the city's gay community and attracts a relaxed trendy crowd. The atmosphere is always welcoming and the cooking dependable.

❺ Cloister of Santi Quattro Coronati ★★
Via dei Santi Quattro Coronati, 20. Mon.-Sat. 9.30am-noon, 4.30-6pm

(Oct.-Mar. only in the morning, except Sat.).

Enter the nave and ring the bell for admittance. Built around 1220, this is a place full of calm beauty, truly an oasis of peace and tranquility in the midst of a busy weekend.

❻ Basilica of Santi Giovanni e Paolo
Open every day 9-11am, 4-5.30pm.

You'll discover an interesting layering of styles and eras here, as the basilica was built on an ancient plot of Roman dwellings, the remains of which are still discernible today. Another example of this can be seen in the basement of one of the houses, where there's a nymphaeum decorated with a very attractive fresco (3rd century AD) depicting what is considered a rare subject in Greek mythology – the return of Proserpina from Hades. The bell-tower, the façade and the side-chapel are from the 12th century, and the interior dates from the 17th century.

❼ VILLA CELIMONTANA GARDENS

Entrance in Piazza della Navicella
Open every day from 7am until dusk.

This charming park contains box trees, exotic trees, hollies, laurels and pines, and is an ideal place for a picnic (unknown to tourists, too). Be sure to see the obelisk brought back from Egypt and dedicated to Ramses II. At the centre of the park is a delightful 16th-century house built for the Dukes of Mattei. Today it serves as the seat of the Italian geographical society.

'Across the Tiber' in Trastevere

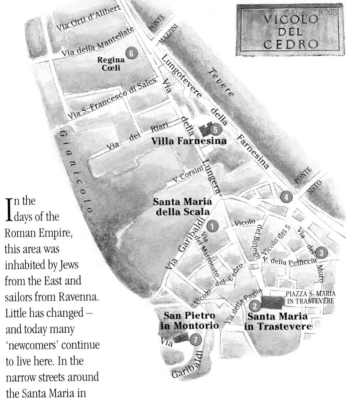

VICOLO
DEL
CEDRO

In the days of the Roman Empire, this area was inhabited by Jews from the East and sailors from Ravenna. Little has changed – and today many 'newcomers' continue to live here. In the narrow streets around the Santa Maria in Trastevere church, the arrival of new residents and upwardly mobile prices are forcing some of the older Roman residents out. It's a pleasant area to wander in during the day and to relax in during the evenings in some of the numerous bars, cafés and restaurants.

❶ Church of Santa Maria della Scala ★

Piazza Santa Maria della Scala.
The multicoloured marble altar with flights of angels rising in adoration is yet another of those breathtaking Baroque effects. You can, on request, visit the old pharmacy where Fra Basilio (1726-1804) invented 'water to cure hysteria', which you can still buy in the shop Monasteri in Piazza delle 5 Lune (see p. 37).

❷ Church of Santa Maria in Trastevere ★★★

Basilica open every day 8am-1pm, 3.30-6pm.

Though rather sleepy during the day, this pedestrian square comes alive at night, when bars and restaurants do good business under the indulgent eye of the Mother and Child. But don't admire the mosaic on the front of the church without seeing the superb examples to be found in the side chapels. Due deference is in order - you are now standing in front of the first Christian building officially open to the cult, in the middle of the 3rd century, though this particular church was rebuilt in the 12th, 17th and 19th centuries.

❸ Guaytamelli ★
Via del Moro, 59
9.30am-1.30pm, 4-8pm

You'll find all the old instruments (hourglasses, sundials, monastic candles, etc.) for measuring time in this charming workshop

owned by Adrien Rodriguez. It's a wonderful place for timeless original presents.

❹ Romolo ★★
Via di Porta Settimania, 8
☎ 06 581 82 84

The house where Raphael's mysterious mistress, known as the *Fornarina* (or baker), once lived has now become a restaurant. It's a lovely place to enjoy a long lunch in the garden, and in the evening it offers a welcome escape from the hubbub of Trastevere. Be sure to try the fresh pasta with artichoke or radish sauce.

❺ Villa Farnesina
Via della Lungara, 30
Mon.-Sat. 9am-1pm.

Agostino Chigi was a rich banker, a humanist and a man interested in astrology. He commissioned Raphael to paint the frescoes in his villa by the Tiber. But Raphael fell in love and did not complete the painting in the loggia illustrating the legend of Cupid and Psyche. He did, however, leave us the magnificent *Triumph of Galatea*.

❻ The surroundings of the Regina Coeli prison ★
Via della Lungara

After enjoying the glorious frescoes in the Farnesina, you have to come back down to earth eventually. Don't be deceived by its name – the Regina Coeli ('the Queen of Heaven') prison is far from a dreamlike place. In fact, it's where hundreds of detainees currently await their trials. It's worth taking a walk around the perimeter where you'll discover some charming streets.

❼ THE TEMPIETTO OF SAN PIETRO IN MONTORIO ★★★
Inside the courtyard of the San Pietro in Montorio convent.
Open every day 9am-noon, 4-6.30pm.

This Renaissance masterpiece by Bramante (1502) is a small circular temple of classical elegance set like a jewel in the courtyard of a convent. Climb a little further to the top of the Janiculum Hill and you'll have a splendid view over the city, a view already admired by Chateaubriand, Stendhal, Taine and Zola.

Rooms and Restaurants

HOTELS

Choosing a hotel in Rome means first of all deciding which part of the city to stay in. As Rome is relatively small and the places of interest quite close together, it's best to stay in the *centro storico*, near Piazza Navona and Piazza di Spagna, the two main tourist centres. Our choice of hotels does not attempt to cover all parts of Rome, and assumes you'd want to be close to the monuments and enjoy getting around on foot.

Hotels are graded on a scale of one to five stars. Roman hotels are scarce and almost all are expensive (around L100,000-400,000 with breakfast) – somewhat of a surprise for a city as popular with tourists. Room prices can vary according to size, even within the same hotel. Prices are set by the state and usually include VAT.

By law, room prices have to be displayed in every room and it is unusual to be able to agree a lower price. Nearly all quality hotels are air-conditioned and, just as vitally, soundproofed.

If you bring a child, expect to pay an additional 10 to 40%, even if you share a room, as prices are only for a double room. If there are four of you, it's probably worthwhile reserving two rooms. If you're bringing a car, find out first if the hotel has parking facilities.

RELIGIOUS INSTITUTIONS

Though you may not be a regular churchgoer, pilgrim or student, you can always try staying in a religious institution. Everyone is welcome (but if you're going as a family make sure you ask whether they accept young children) and such places have basic comfort (no en-suite bathrooms). A word of warning – they're popular with school groups. You won't pay a lot for your lodgings, but you will have to be back in the early evening (usually before 9 or 10pm).

In the vicinity of the Vatican try:
Domus Mariae, Via Aurelia, 481 ☎ 06 662 3138, or
Madri Pie, Via A. de Gasperi, 4 ☎ 06 63 1967.

WHEN TO BOOK

If you're intending to stay in Rome in September or October, at Christmas or

Easter, or in May or June, it's a good idea to make reservations, unless you're coming with a package deal.

If you're reserving from home, do so by telephone and confirm by fax at least one month, if not two, in advance (i.e. avoid relying on the postal service). To be sure your reservation is taken seriously, send an advance payment or give your credit card number. If you arrive in Rome without having made a reservation, go to a tourist information office and they will provide you with information about rooms in your price range.

On arrival at the hotel, you'll be asked for your passport to fill in the register (a legal requirement). Make sure you ask for the swift return of your passport as you should always make sure it is safe. It may also be required if you want to change money. On the day of your departure, you'll be expected to vacate the room by noon at the latest. If you

MEAL TIMES

Lunch usually starts between 1.30pm and 2pm, dinner towards 9pm. Many restaurants close in August, and are often closed on Sunday evenings and on Mondays. It's best to reserve for Saturday dinner and Sunday lunch.

expect to leave early in the morning, ask to have the bill prepared in advance.

As regards tipping, it isn't customary to tip the head porter, though it is recommended at meals in restaurants, as service is never included. The usual amount is 10 to 15% of the bill.

RESTAURANTS

Eating in Rome is obviously no longer as lavish as in the time of the ancient Romans. Nowadays tastes are simpler, but the best seasonal ingredients tend to be used. There are several broad categories of eating

establishment, most notably the *trattoria*, an unassuming establishment offering traditional family cooking, and the more sophisticated, and consequently more expensive, *ristorante*. Prices nevertheless remain affordable (usually L30,000-L60,000). In general, you should expect to add a L3,000 cover charge per person.

ROMAN SPECIALITIES

Meat and fish dishes are served without vegetables, which need to be ordered separately. Remember that in Italy pasta is considered a starter and not a main course in itself. It's best to avoid anywhere too close to tourist centres, such as St Peter's or the Roman Forum (you're likely to eat badly and prices are exorbitant). The best place for typical Roman cooking is the area around the abattoirs of Testaccio and in the Ghetto. Romans normally drink white wine, which comes from the Alban Hills (20km/12 miles from Rome) and is served in pitchers. The best-known wine is Frascati, which is made from the Trebbiano grape. Marino is fruity, white Colli Lanuvini is very dry and slightly bitter, and Vignanello is sparkling. Galestro is currently a popular white wine and comes from Tuscany. Red wines are usually from Tuscany and include Chianti, Brunello di Montalcino (very expensive at L20,000) and Vino Nobile di Montepulciano. That said, one of the best Italian wines is Barolo, which comes from Piedmont.

HOTELS

Aventine district

Sant'Anselmo
★★★

Piazza Sant'Anselmo, 2
☎ 06 574 35 47
fax 06 578 36 04
L180,000-L350,000
Book well in advance.

A charming villa deep in the leafy peace and quiet of the Aventine

Hill, behind Piazza Cavalieri di Malta. When the weather is fine, breakfast is served in the garden. Stencilled flowers decorate the ceiling of the reception. 46 spacious rooms in individual styles, perhaps a little over-decorated, but quite tastefully furnished.

Campo dei Fiori

Teatro di Pompei ★★★

Largo del Pallaro, 8
☎ 06 687 28 12
fax 06 688 05 531
Around L250,000
Air-conditioned.

A small, welcoming hotel (12 rooms) much appreciated by

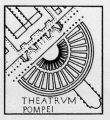

THEATRVM POMPEI

highbrow tourists. Simply furnished, with prints on the walls, terracotta floors, and exposed beams. Last but not least, the staff are most attentive.

Campo dei Fiori ★★

Via del Biscione, 6
☎ 06 688 06865
fax 06 687 60 03
L120,000-L150,000.

This small hotel (27 rooms) won the 'Oscar' in the Gambero Rosso guidebook. The 6th-floor terrace has a view onto the Pantheon and Campo dei Fiori. This is a tasteful, unpretentious hotel, popular with the film world and decorated in painted wood and metal, with imitation stained-glass windows, wall-to-wall carpeting and scented (it seems) by Crabtree & Evelyn.

Sole

Via del Biscione, 76
☎ 06 68 80 68 73
fax 06 689 37 87
L130,000-L180,000.

This is one of Rome's oldest hotels and has retained its charm by avoiding refurbishment. It feels more like a private residence than a hotel. There's a cat, free to roam the premises, as time ticks slowly by. There's also a small terrace garden with a view over the rooftops of the city. Try to reserve rooms 13 or 14.

HOTEL TEATRO DI POMPEO

Capitol

Forum ★★★★

Via Tor de Conti, 25
☎ 06 679 24 46
fax 06 678 64 79

L300,000-L520,000. This is an elegant hotel with an old-fashioned charm located in the heart of Ancient Rome and housed in a palazzo made from materials recycled from the Imperial Forum. The rooms have all mod cons and are soundproofed. The roof restaurant has a panoramic view and is one of the most delightful in Rome.

HOTEL FORUM

Celian Hill

Celio ★★★

Via dei S. Quattro, 35c
☎ 06 70 49 53 33
fax 06 709 63 77
L200,000-L350,000.

Located in a quiet, working-class area not far from the Colosseum, this hotel is surprisingly elegant and has a hushed atmosphere. Breakfast is served in the rooms.

convince you you were eating outdoors.

Piazza Navona

Dei Portoghesi
★★★

Via dei Portoghesi, 1
☎ 06 686 42 31
fax 06 687 69 76
L190,000-270,000.

Ideally located between Piazza Navona and Piazza di Spagna, this simple, slightly old-fashioned hotel is nevertheless extremely comfortable. The roof terrace looks onto the Portuguese church and a statue of a monkey once said to have performed a miracle.

Pantheon

Del Sole al Pantheon ★★★★
Piazza della Rotonda, 63
☎ 06 678 04 41
fax 06 69 94 06 89
L360,000-L500,000.

The hotel dates back to 1467, and is superbly located in front

Piazza di Spagna

Inghilterra ★★★★
Via Bocca di Leone, 14
☎ 06 699 81
fax 06 69 92 22 43
L570,000-L660,000
Air-conditioned.

Opened in 1850, this establishment has had many famous

guests, most notably Liszt and Hemingway, and remains much in demand. All rooms are individually decorated. The *trompe-l'oeil* frescoes on the dining room ceiling could almost

of the Pantheon. It has of course been renovated since, but always with luxury in mind. Today not only do most of the rooms have panelled or ornamental ceilings, they also have a jacuzzi. Many illustrious guests have stayed here, from Ariosto to Sartre.

panelling, soft lighting, thick carpets and heavy curtains. The luxury extends as far as travertine

marble bathrooms, rather reminiscent of the old Roman baths. Good value for money.

Piazza del Popolo

Valadier ★★★★

Via della Fontanella, 15
☎ 06 361 05 92
fax 06 320 15 58
Around L370,000
(L330,000 at weekends)
Air-conditioned.

The Valadier is one of the 'designer' hotels – to be included alongside the Royalton in New York by Starck and the Costes by Jacques Garcia in Paris. Expect to find marble surfaces, exotic wood

Locarno ★★

Via della Penna, 22
☎ 06 361 08 41
fax 06 321 52 49
L330-360,000 for a double room
Air-conditioned.

This is a former guesthouse in a small, lively street near the Tiber. Decorated in 1920s style, with an Art Nouveau entrance and a Tiffany lamp in reception. It also has a pleasant patio with a cool, soothing fountain. Ask for a room facing the courtyard to avoid the noise.

Trevi

Fontana ★★★

Piazza di Trevi, 96
☎ 06 678 61 13
Around L315,000 for a double room
Air-conditioned.

This exquisite hotel occupies a 14th-century monastery located opposite the famous fountain. Rooms with a view cost an extra L20,000 but do note that they are not air-conditioned due to a law imposed by the Italian commission for historic monuments. However,

these rooms do have perfectly adequate old-fashioned ventilators instead.

Piazza di Spagna

Mozart ★★★

Via dei Greci, 23
☎ 06 69 94 00 41
fax 06 67 84 22 71
Around L225,000 for a
double room
Air-conditioned.

An attractive place to stay despite the somewhat small bathrooms (with shower). The breakfast room opens onto the stone-paved reception hall.

Vatican-Prati

Columbus ★★★

Via della Conciliazione, 33
☎ 06 686 54 35
fax 06 686 48 74
Around L370,000 for a
double room.

This hotel occupies a 15th-century palazzo near the Vatican. The original dining hall has now been converted into the reception. High ceilings, wrought-iron chandeliers, a massive marble fireplace, a veranda with frescoes and a lovely private garden all make this a stunning place to stay.

Via Veneto

Eden ★★★★

Via Ludovisi, 49
☎ 06 474 35 51
fax 06 482 15 84
L400,000-
L700,000
Air conditioned
Roof garden.

Founded in 1889 by a German called Nistelweck, and designed in an attractive neo-Classical style by the architect Settimi, this luxury hotel was totally renovated in 1994. The Eden offers exquisite elegance, and is finished with period pieces and marble-tiled bathrooms.

HOTEL EDEN
ROME

RESTAURANTS

Aventine

Trattoria San Teodoro

Via dei Fienili, 49
☎ 06 687 09 33
Closed Sun. and in the summer
Around L35,000.

Romantic paintings hang on the walls of this picturesque restaurant in the old city. The owner is an ex-hippy, who has now turned his hand to running a restaurant. Simple cuisine, but with a great variety of ingredients for salads, and ideas on how to spice up sardines or cod.

Perilli

Via Marmorata, 53
☎ 06 574 24 15
Open every day except Wed.
12.30-3pm and 7.30-11pm.
Closed in August.

This is a typically noisy and

friendly Roman restaurant, but with little attention paid to decor. The authentic cooking is served in generous portions. Try the *praetoriana* escalopes, a speciality of the house and a good choice on a warm summer evening. Expect to pay around L50,000.

Campo dei Fiori

Santa Barbara

Largo dei Librari
Around L50,000.

This little neon-lit bistrot is located on a small piazza at the end of Via dei Giubonnari. The unattractive floor tiles and cloying odour of fried food can be a little off-putting, but it is worth a trip for the truly divine deep-fried cod filet (*filetti di baccalà*) with salad.

Caffetteria Poppea

Via dei Chiavari, 62
☎ 06 68 80 19 50
Until 3am, closed Mon.

Under the bizarrely-lit plexiglass floor, you can just make out Roman ruins. The stencilled wall motifs imitating the frescoes at Pompeii, and the artificially-faded tints of the furnishings, make this bistrot one of the best in the area.

L'Angolo Divino

Via dei Balestrari, 12
☎ 06 686 44 13
Around L20,000.

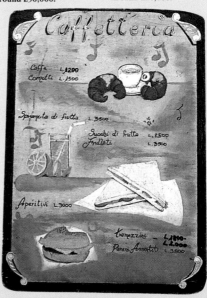

Situated alongside the Palazzo Farnese, this former grocer's shop (now a wine bar) is an ideal place to stop for a snack. Massimo Crippa and his brothers have bought up a wide selection of wines, which can be tried at any time of the day with some excellent charcuterie or cheese. The quiche is home-made.

La Carbonara

Piazza Campo dei Fiori, 3
☎ 06 686 47 83
Closed Tue.
Around L50,000.

When the weather is good, this two-storey restaurant sets up its tables on the Campo dei Fiori.

In the past it used to be a haunt of Pasolini, the writer and film-maker who caught so well the poetry and violence of 1960s Rome. The house speciality is pasta with broccoli sauce. Excellent wine list.

Grotte teatro di Pompeo

Via del Biscione, 73
☎ 06 68 80 36 86
Closed Mon.
Around L40,000.

What makes this restaurant unusual is that it's housed in the basement of Rome's first theatre to be built of stone – though only the theatre walls remain. The cooking is unpretentious, but it's always worth asking if there are any dishes available that are not shown on the menu as you may discover something unusual.

Celian Hill

OrazioVia di Porta Latina, 5
☎ 06 70 49 24 01
Closed Tue. and Aug.
Around L50,000.

This restaurant nestles amidst greenery behind the Celian Hill near the Baths of Caracalla. It's ideal for a meal *all'aperto* (on the terrace). Dishes include juicy lasagne and spicy *tagliolini alla matriciana*.

Historic centre

La Taverna da Giovanni

Via del Banco di Santo Spirito, 58
☎ 06 686 15 12
Closed Mon.
Around L45,000.

This medieval-style tavern is a fitting place to eat after a visit to the Castel Sant'Angelo. The charcuterie comes from the Abbruzzi and the roast lamb (*abbachio laziale arrosto*) and various cod dishes are delicious.

Ai Tre Scalini

Via dei S. Quattro, 30

☎ 06 709 63 09
Closed Mon. and Aug.
Around L70,000.

Rossana and Matteo have invented a new subtle-flavoured dish – gnocchi with nettles. In the guidebook published by *Espresso*, a national weekly magazine, this restaurant receives glowing praise.

Acchiappafantas mi Pizzeria

Via dei Cappellari, 66
☎ 06 687 34 62
Closed Tue. and Aug.
Around L25,000.

The *margherita* pizza was invented in Naples in 1830 by a *pizzaiolo* (pizza chef) as a tribute to Marguerite of Savoy. In her honour he created a pizza in the colours of the Italian flag. He used tomato for the red, mozzarella for the white and basil for the green. The story is recounted on the walls of this pizzeria popular with young people, where you can eat well without spending a fortune (open in the evenings).

Ricciutelli Ada

**Osteria con cucina,
Via dei Banchi Nuovi, 14**
Around L20,000.

We advise you to go out and seek out Ada while you still can — before this old tavern is turned into a soulless snack bar for a trendy clientele. With its wooden benches, marble tables, formica sideboard and distinctive tang of wine in the air, it's not short of atmosphere. Come here to enjoy the feel of how Rome must once have been as much (if not more than) for the cuisine.

Ghetto

Sora Lella

Via Ponte Quattro Capi, 16
☎ 06 686 16 01
Closed Sun. and Aug.

It's a good idea to book first if you want to have dinner in this historic restaurant. The cooking may not always be excellent but the wine list and the service are. The specialities are filling *romaneschi* (Roman) dishes, such as *rigatoni alla pajata* and *coda alla vaccinara*. Expect to pay around L70,000.

Evangelista

Via delle Zoccolette, 11
☎ 06 687 58 10
Closed Sun. and Aug.
Around L60,000.

Try the fried artichokes and also the Tuscan wines served from a traditional *fiasco*. Though the word *fiasco* means 'failure', this container was an immediate

success. Its traditional decorative and protective covering was made using a plant that only grows in the small lakes of the Val d'Arno in Tuscany. The fiasco first appeared in the 11th century, and in 1574 its capacity was fixed at 2.28 litres. It should only ever contain Tuscan wine.

Trastevere

Il Ciak

Vicolo del Cinque, 21
☎ 06 589 47 74
Closed Aug.
Booking advisable.

This is a small Tuscan 'enclave' frequented by a media crowd. Here you'll find excellent sautéed seafood and ravioli served in a different sauce every day. Wines are reasonably priced, and the friendly and efficient service is overseen by Paolo Celli, the chef and owner.

Ripa 12

Via San Francesco a Ripa, 12
☎ 06 580 90 93
Closed Sun. and 15-31 Aug.

This is the place for whole grilled fish served with simple sauces that bring out the full flavour. The fresh anchovy salad and fish carpaccio (salmon, swordfish or bass) confirm the talents of a true Trastevere chef. Expect to pay L55,000.

San Callisto

Piazza San Callisto, 9
☎ 06 581 47 38
Closed at lunchtimes.

Pizzerias are perfect for a simple meal in a lively, informal setting. According to purists, the pizza should be prepared using only simple ingredients – water, flour, salt, yeast for the pizza dough, tomato paste and mozzarella. When taken out of the oak-fired oven, the pizza

should be thin and circular with crusty edges.

L'Isola Felice

Vicolo del Leopardo, 39
☎ 06 581 47 38
Closed Aug.
Around L30,000.

Anna and Wilma are the two cooks in this trattoria in a lovely part of Trastevere. Anna is originally from Sardinia and

has specialised in *culurgiones*, a simple dish made with secret ingredients and eaten with a Prosecco (sparkling white wine). Be sure to try these new tastes.

Pantheon

Fortunato

Via del Pantheon, 55
☎ 06 679 27 88
Closed Sun. and 15-31 Aug.
Around L60,000.

The Fortunato is popular with politicians, their bodyguards and journalists, whom you can come here to observe at close quarters. Though the restaurant is very fashionable, the cooking can, on occasion, suffer from a rather careless attitude.

La Caffetteria

Piazza di Pietra, 65
☎ 06 679 81 47
Closed Sun. in the summer, 7am-9pm in Aug.

This is a good place to come for a speedy lunch. Try the pizza *di scarola* (chicory) or have a *sformato di maccheroni* (baked pasta with grated cheese). The desserts are divine – try the *sfogliatella* or the *pasticiotto*. All amidst faded elegance and with old-style service.

Antica Taverna

Via Monte Giordano, 12
☎ 06 68 80 10 53.

This *trattoria* has a warm atmosphere and offers a fixed price menu (L40,000) that includes wine. Choose the menu and Paolo and Michele will give you some *bruschetta* (toasted bread rubbed with garlic and tomatoes), an *assaggio di pasta* (three different types of pasta) and a *secondo* (a main dish) of your choice.

L'Orso

Via del Orso, 33
☎ 06 686 49 04
Closed Mon. and Aug.
Around L65,000.

A friendly setting and very respectable Abbruzzo cooking at moderate prices. And for those of you whose stomachs have a tendency to rumble – the *antipasti* are served as soon as you sit down.

Da Giuseppe al 59

Via Angelo Brunetti, 59
☎ 06 321 90 19
Closed Sun.
Around L60,000.

Here you'll find certain lesser-known regional specialities: sautéed courgette (zucchini) flowers, the classic *misticanza* (Roman name for mixed salad), stewed squid with tomatoes, and saffron peppers, served swiftly in elegant surroundings.

La Buca Di Ripetta

Via di Ripetta, 36
☎ 06 321 93 91

Closed Mon., Sun. eve. and Aug.
Once the haunt of artists living in the Rue Margutta, this

restaurant still serves unfussy, inexpensive fare. The speciality here is *saltimbocca alla Romana* (wrapped veal escalope with ham and sage). Expect to pay around L40,000.

Fiaschetteria Beltrame

Via della Croce, 39
☎ 06 67 90 03 Closed Sun.
L40,000.

As the signed paintings and photographs on the walls testify, this was once the restaurant of the artists of old Rome. Here they serve good-quality, perfectly-cooked traditional dishes in a homely atmosphere. Expect rapid service but don't expect to linger.

Nino

Via Borgognona, 11
☎ 06 679 56 76
Closed Sun. and Aug.

High ceilings and dark wood panelling, together with the ancient Roman scene depicted on the window separating the kitchen from the dining room, conspire to lend a certain charm to this well-established restaurant. The buffet of *antipasti* is excellent. Try the courgettes (zucchini) with melted cheese, the ravioli stuffed with white truffles, or the *pappardelle*

This Neapolitan restaurant offers about 100 dishes, all equally good. All the wine and all the ingredients are brought in from Naples. Good value for money (L50,000).

Via Veneto

Cantina Cantarini
Piazza Sallustio, 12
☎ 06 485 528
Closed Sun., 15-31 Aug. and Christmas.

This is a popular local *trattoria* tucked away on a small square and serving excellent food. Meat is served from Mon. to Fri. (L30,000) and fish on other days. The specialities are from the Marche region: vegetables and *fritto misto* (squid and shrimps). And the good mood of the waiters is thrown in for free.

(which are wider than tagliatelle) with hare sauce. Around L60,000.

Otello
Via della Croce, 81
☎ 06 678 14 54
Closed Sun.
Set meal L36,000.

During the week this is a meeting place for members of the Roman fashion world, who congregate on the charming and discreet terrace between 1 and 3pm. Serves tasty traditional dishes, such as *melanzane alla parmigiana* (aubergine/eggplant gratin).

Vatican-Prati

Dal Toscano
Via Germanico, 56-58
☎ 06 39 72 57 17
Closed Mon., Aug. and Christmas
Around L50,000.

If you can't survive the weekend without a good steak, this is the place to come. They also have other Tuscan specialities such as *fagioli al fiasco* (white beans) and sautéed mushrooms.

Lorodinapoli

Via Fabio Massimo, 101
☎ 06 323 57 90
Closed Sun. eve. and Mon.

Colline Emiliane
Via Avignonesi, 22
☎ 06 481 75 38
Closed Fri. and Aug.

The name is a misnomer as the food here is not from the Emiglia region but from the Marche. It's a regular rendez-vous for locals in the know. The decor is bare but it's worth paying the high price for the sautéed clams and beef marrow *risotto* served up by the chef with great panache. Around L40,000.

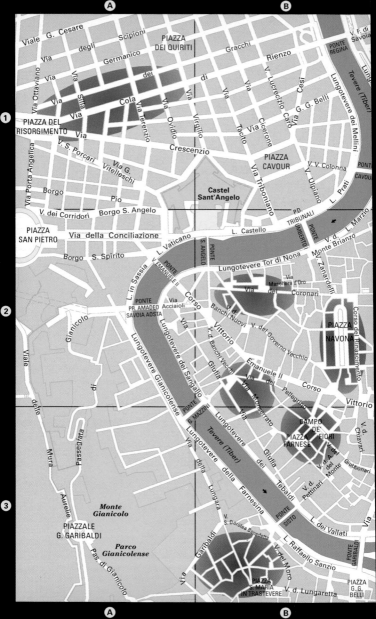

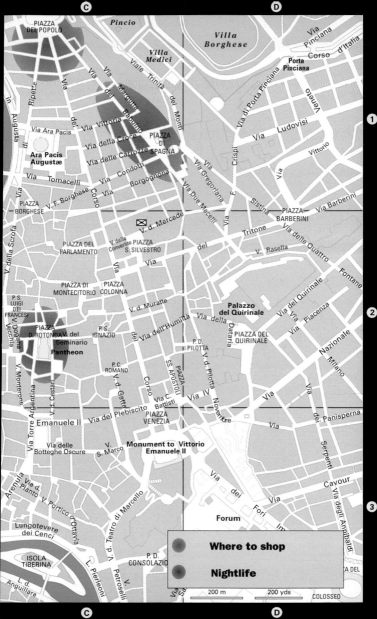

shopping in Rome

Rome is an expensive city, so don't expect to find too many bargains. Nevertheless, window shopping is a joy and you will find good value for money, especially if buying leather goods (shoes, bags, gloves and belts) and certain decorative items (lamps, Italian modern designer goods and glassware).

OPENING HOURS

Shops usually open 9am-1pm and 3.30-7.30pm (4-8pm in Summer), except on Sundays and Monday mornings. Grocery shops also close on Thursday afternoons. Some bookshops (where people often meet) and some clothes shops (around Campo dei Fiori, for example) open on Sundays, 10am or 3-7pm. August is traditionally the month when small businesses take their annual holiday. In Rome, most shops and restaurants close for about two weeks around 15 August.

REAL AND NOT-SO-REAL SALES

'Sales' last from about mid-July to mid-September, and from Christmas to March, in other words, about six months of the year. In actual fact, such sales comprise 15-20% reductions on certain items only. Sometimes the reductions can be as much as 50%, but most often these occur on designer articles which, even when heavily discounted, remain expensive. By law, the label should always show both the original price and the sale price. As for the *vendite promozionali* (special introductory sales) and *sconti* (discounts) that you see splashed in enormous letters across shop windows, these are usually no more than tricks to entice customers into the shops, whose windows are usually completely obscured.

That's no reason not to go inside, but you're unlikely to find a good bargain.

DEPARTMENT STORES

La Rinascente (Via del Corso, 189) was the first department store to open in Rome in 1887. It took its current name in 1917 when it was called this by the famous Italian poet Gabriele D'Annunzio after a serious fire, *(Rinascente* means 'that is reborn'). The glass and metal architecture by De Angelis has remained unchanged. Rinascente is the most upmarket store in Rome and prices are not cheap. Nevertheless, it is worth going there for off-the-peg clothes, household linen, luggage and the perfume counters. The men's section is well-stocked and offers a good selection of ties and shirts.

Coin (Piazzale Appio, 7) is located in the San Giovanni district (Metro San Giovanni). There's no food hall, but there's a good clothes section, especially for children, and they also sell quite attractive crockery and household articles.

Standa sells everything, from food to fitness equipment, and from toys to hi-fi. The largest outlet is near Via Cola di Rienzo. Though the store often has good value discounts (e.g. for swimsuits, towards the end of the season), prices are generally high for the quality on offer.

Upim is the most popular department store and doesn't really have any branches in the *centro storico* (the historic city centre). It mainly sells clothes, which, though not always well-cut, are nonetheless of average quality and cheap.

WHERE TO GO FOR WHAT

The area around Piazza di Spagna is where to find the

FINDING YOUR WAY

Alongside the addresses in the Shopping and Nightlife sections we have shown the grid references relating to the map on pages 78-9.

boutiques (for ladies' suits, jewellery, shoes, etc.) – Valentino, Gucci, Fendi (which takes up a large tract of Via Borgognona), Missoni and Armani are all to be found within a short distance of one another. The more prestigious antique shops, as well as several smart restaurants, are to be found in Via Margutta, and contemporary designers and stylists in Via del Babuino.

Rome really is an exciting place to shop. Don't expect to find shopping centres or malls though, Italian shopping is centred around small, individual stores and

boutiques and you will receive more personal attention from the shopkeeper or store assistant who will be keen to help you.

MARKETS

The larger and more colourful and lively markets in the centre of Rome are worth a visit. They usually open 7am-1pm, Monday to Saturday. Only the Porta Portese flea market is open on Sundays, 6.30am-2pm.

Rome's oldest market is held on Campo dei Fiori (meaning 'Flora's Courtyard' and not 'flower market', as might be imagined. Flora was the mistress of the great Roman general, Pompey). Here you will find the best fish in the city, fresh vegetables and attractively-piled fruit, as well as kitchen utensils, tablecloths and toys.

On the other side of Corso Vittorio are two smaller food markets – the Pace market, where showbiz stars, Roman aristocrats and other local residents shop, and, near the Pantheon, the market on Piazza delle Coppelle, which, with its backdrop of ochre houses and sun-faded parasols, seems like something straight out of a painting by the 19th-century artist Corot.

HOW TO PAY

It's probably easiest to pay for everything in cash if possible.

Credit cards and traveller's cheques are accepted only in the larger shops (as indicated by small stickers affixed to the window). Try to avoid paying

in foreign currency as the exchange rate is unlikely to be favourable.

For every transaction you make, you should be given a *ricevuta fiscale*, a receipt (the penalty otherwise is a fine), which you should keep. It is in any case necessary as you could be asked to show it at customs, and will be useful if you decide to re-sell any items, or for an insurance claim in the event of a burglary.

If you buy any works of art, you are entitled to request a certificate of authenticity.

Prices are usually clearly marked in shops and bargaining is only customary at the flea market or in secondhand shops, where you may be given a 20-30% discount, but only after long, ritual negotiations.

SHIPPING GOODS HOME

Usually, if you buy a piece of furniture or other unwieldy item, the shop will be able to arrange delivery. Many antique dealers regularly use international hauliers, who will give you a quote based on the distance and the volume of goods to be transported. Prices are around L250-400,000 per m^3 (35cuft), and delivery may take 25-30 days. In case the dealers can't help you try:

**Bolinger,
Via dei Buonvisi, 61
☎ 06 655 71 61.**

**Gondrand
(specialist in works of art),
Via Idronore della
Magliana, 163
☎ 06 657 463 40.**

WOMEN'S FASHION

For the fashion-conscious amongst you, Rome has many pleasures in store, though its private showrooms offer unique creations at astronomic prices, the designer boutiques around Piazza di Spagna are exquisite and there are also ready-to-wear labels catering to the shallower pocket, and collections for the young. Rome has it all.

Prada
Via Condotti, 93 (C1)
☎ 06 67 90 897.

Miuccia Prada is bringing back a style of clothing drawing on 1970s fashions. Go up to the first floor, if only to admire one of the city's most exquisite views over Piazza di Spagna. No doubt partly to enhance the decor of absinthe-green walls, a guard in military-style uniform patrols among the throng of excited (usually) Japanese shoppers. You'll find a bit of everything here: clothes (two million lire for a jacket), bags and shoes (for L400,000). The style is sober, almost minimalist chic. The same is true of the men's line, but the quality is always unbeatable.

Fendissime
Via Fontanella Borghese, 56A (C1)
☎ 06 687 62 90.

This is the Fendi label at its best, a more youthful look designed by the most recent generation of Fendi

sisters. The ready-to-wear label is designed by Karl Lagerfeld. The boutique itself is a must, and uses all kinds of ideas from recent painting exhibitions in its somewhat highbrow window displays. You may find yourself tempted by leatherette trousers for L160,000, T-shirts for L100,000. And why not – you won't find anything like this back home.

Ballester
Via del Corso, 410-411 (C2)
☎ 06 66 87 14 54.

This long-established boutique has been given an attractive new look that has kept the Art Deco ceiling paintings and harmonised them with a floor mosaic and pale wood furnishings. All the major

labels, such as Fendi Sweesh, are here, and the clothes on offer are stylish leisurewear for all occasions. Whether you're looking for a suit, a pair of trousers, a skirt or a jacket, you're sure to find something you like.

Versace Jean's
Via Frattina, 116 (C1)
☎ 06 678 76 80.

Despite all the bronzes, the Empire furniture, the mosaics on the floor

and the moulded ceiling, this is not an antique shop. This is in fact the exquisite Versace boutique and well worth seeking out. Here you'll find designer jeans in all sizes (and doing justice to the female form), as well as T-shirts and shirts to go with them. Of course, it won't be cheap, but the quality is guaranteed.

Sermonetta
Corso Vittorio Emanuelle II, 43 (B2)
☎ 06 679 46 89.

Roman women are forever walking by this shop on Largo Argentino waiting for the first hint of a sale. Like the interior decor, the collections are classic, soberly-cut, and made from the finest materials. The jackets and skirts are certain to be a perfect fit, so even if the sales haven't yet started, why not go on in and treat yourself?

Nia
Via Vittoria , 48 (C1)
☎ 06 679 51 98.

If a Roman woman had to recommend just one place for buying clothes, this would be it. The clothes here are the work of young designers and are all wearable items in bespoke soft and satiny materials – washed silk, slinky knitwear and flowing, milk-white viscose. Altogether a very attractive collection – discreetly elegant yet not too conventional, in other words, just what you'd expect from Italian designers. A plain crepe dress sells for L350,000.

Halfon
Via del Corso, 507-508 (C2)
☎ 06 679 09 93.

This chain of shops sells reasonably-priced clothes based on

classic designs. Here you can find almost perfectly-cut ladies' suits (with short or long jacket, buttons or zip) which, if worn with the right seasonal colours and designer accessories, could well pass off for something it isn't. Sleeveless dresses sell for L120,000, and shorts for L30,000.

Discount della Moda
Via Gesu e Maria, 16 (C1)
☎ 06 361 37 96.

The concept of discount shops hasn't yet caught on in the *centro storico*. Nevertheless, this designer seconds shop sells end-of-collection designer clothes at a

50% discount. It's rather more conventional and uninspiring than its London counterparts and prices vary enormously.

Paola Vassarotti

Vicolo della Cuccagna, 12 (B2)
☎ 06 689 32 09.

This boutique is hidden away down a few steps in a narrow street parallel to Piazza Navona. Here you'll find not only clothes made from the finest materials (silk, linen, etc.) and a wide choice of handmade knitwear at very reasonable prices (e.g. a long dress in jersey wool for L120,000), you'll also find last season's

A lady's spring suit sells for a million lire.

Tartarughe

Via Pie di Marmo, 17 (C2)
☎ 06 66 79 22 40.

This shop (whose name means 'Tortoises') close to the Pantheon, sells both ready-to-wear and made-to-measure clothes for women who like their appearance to be a little out of the ordinary. You'll find novel suits, beautiful evening dresses, and even made-to-measure wedding dresses, as well as all the accessories you need. If you're after an outfit for a special occasion,

you might find something here, though check your bank balance first.

Tower

Piazza dell'Unita, 57 (A1)
☎ 06 32 11 66 37.

In this shop, L550,000 will buy you a linen suit with a cotton and linen sleeveless jumper, and L100,000 a plain but pretty, close-fitting dress. In other words, Tower may not necessarily look like much, but does offer good-quality basic essentials at inexpensive prices. The materials are attractive, and the cut sober yet elegant. Worth a visit.

Gente

Via del Babuino, 82 (C2),
Via Cola di Rienzo, 277 (A1), Via Frattina, 69 (C1)
☎ 06 63 21 15 16/06 66 78 91 32/06 63 20 76 71.

This chain of shops knows its product, cool clothes by young designers sold amidst new wave decor to trendy Roman girls with money to spend. They sell all

---

SIZES

While you are busy hunting for that incredibly chic little black number, don't forget that clothes sizes in Italy are different from those at home (for both women and men). Most sales assistants should be able to assist you in finding the perfect fit, but we have compiled easy reference conversion tables on p.126 to ensure that the outfit of your dreams not only looks amazing but also fits well.

Eres swimwear. Though there may be nothing fancy about this place, it sells nothing but superb clothing.

Moschino

Borgognona, 32A (C1)
☎ 06 678 11 44.

Moschino makes clothes for the young at heart. The high-cut belted jacket with fluorescent collar, the nylon two-tone trousers, are particularly exhibitionist in style. Nevertheless, it's worth dropping by if you're already in the area.

kinds of things to take your fancy – including genuinely innovative clothing, headscarves and footwear – though prices can be a little high. The shop in Via del Babuino is the most offbeat.

Tortuga
Via del Corso, 39-40 (C1)
☎ **06 36 00 18 60.**

Make sure you visit this shop decked out in an Indiana Jones theme. Amongst the lianas, rapids and stuffed crocodiles, you could find exactly the clothes you need for going on safari or taking a cruise up the Nile. The style here is sporty, young and trendy. There's also a choice of exotic objects and plenty of ideas for presents, perhaps even for yourself.

A FORCE OF NATURE

Though you wouldn't know it to look at one, the silkworm is a hard worker. To build its cocoon, a silk envelope protecting the future butterfly, the silkworm will need to produce a string of 'saliva' over half a mile (almost a kilometre) long. After these strings have been collected, stretched and spun, and rid of their 'grit', a single millimetre ($1/32$in) thick string can support a 45kg/99lb weight. And considering 120 strings are needed per centimetre ($3/8$in) of satin crepe, you can see why this kind of material wears so well.

Arsenale
Via del Governo Vecchio, 64 (B2)
☎ **06 686 13 80**

Amidst the understated displays and tasteful wood fittings, you'll find clothes by young designers at reasonable prices. Here you can browse at your leisure along uncrowded display racks, admiring colour and materials, and listening to the (often Italian) background music. It's also a good place to add to your collection of costume jewellery, handbags and shoes.

Marina Rinaldi
Via Boccea, 53 and Via dei Condotti/ Largo Goldoni, 43 (C1)
☎ **06 69 20 04 87.**

Why is it that clothes sizes seem to be getting smaller and smaller – you try on everything in the shop and nothing fits. Well, this won't be the problem here. This particular Italian designer specialises in classic, well-cut clothes in Italian size 44 (UK size 16, USA size 14) and above that won't make you feel about ten years older. At long last a welcoming and affordable shop for women with a real figure!

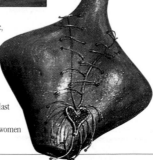

STYLE AND HAUTE COUTURE

The major Italian designers are famous throughout the world for their inimitable chic and refined and relaxed sophistication. Even though Italian haute couture has slowly given way to Italian ready-to-wear, the machine stitches still look handmade and the clothes continue to be cut on the bias, the method used in the 1930s for the most flattering fit. Only the best will do.

Giorgio Armani
Via dei Condotti, 77 (C1)
☎ 06 699 14 60.

Alitalia, which has always had a refined image, has now provided its female staff with a uniform designed by Armani. The ground staff wear natural colours, ranging from brown to sand, those working in the air wear moss-green and olive-green, and the blue jackets are reserved for the hostesses that take care of VIP travellers.

Hepburn, and his workroom is to be visited with appropriate reverence. His use of ink and asphalt-coloured taffetas, velvet and other heavy fabrics allows the cut of the clothes to be very structured, though he is also capable of adding curves by following the new body forms available thanks to stretch fabrics such as stretch chiffon and stretch silk.

Capucci
Via Gregoriana, 56 (D1)
☎ 06 678 36 00
By appointment only.

Capucci was to Catherine Spaack what Givenchy was to Audrey

Gattinoni
Piazza di Spagna, 91 (C1)
☎ 06 679 53 61.

Amidst the serene minimalism and white curtains are Gattinoni's simple flowing styles, in satiny textures and half-tones.

Gai Mattiolo
Via Borgognona, 29 (C1)
☎ 06 559 26 86.

This is a sumptuous boutique decorated in pale woods, pastel tones, and soft indirect lighting playing off small parasols to create intricate patterns of light and shadow. This unique designer is also known as the 'Button King' because of his predilection for interesting and exotic buttons.

Valentino
Via Condotti, 13 (C1)
☎ 06 678 36 56.

An immense red-carpeted stairway leads up to the first floor, where small spartan items of oak and aluminium furniture serve as mounts for the displays. Sober, elegant clothing. Very expensive.

Sorella Fontana
Salita S. Sebastianello (not on map)
☎ 06 63 34 01 57.

This very distinguished boutique is fitted out for a select few, with parchment-wrapped columns, Prussian blue carpets and an ivory stucco ceiling. The bold mix of colours here creates a showy, technicolour style.

Egon von Furstenberg
Via Farnesina, 6 (B3)
☎ 06 63 34 01 57.

Everything appears as if created for the first time in the work of this designer, who is also the grandson of Gianni Agnelli and the brother of Ira von Furstenberg. The dresses are very wearable, even if the style is provocative and the colours over-the-top. Clothes for that glamourous, jet-set look. He also sells clothes via his mail order catalogue *Postal Market*.

Moschino
Via Borgognona, 32A (C1)
☎ 06 678 11 44.

The shop is on two floors and attracts a relatively young set of faithful clients. Haute couture is on the first floor, and luxury ready-to-wear below. Amidst the

over-the-top decor – white lacquer walls, ancient columns and tall mirrors – you're certain to spot the suit you want. However, it will cost at least L900,000 and over a million lire if you want the finest quality.

Rocco Barocco
Via Bocca di Leone, 65A (C1)
☎ 06 679 79 14.

Barocco injects new life into the classics. Perhaps because he's intentionally somewhat

audacious in his use of glamorous colours, his clothes sell like hot cakes in the world of show business. Take a walk on the wild side.

Dolce & Gabbana
Via Borgognona, 7D (C1).
☎ 06 678 29 90.

A surprising and youthful style, somewhat reminiscent of designs by Jean-Paul Gaultier. The shelves are full of plastic materials, ethnic fabrics and vinyl. Very cool and trendy.

MEN'S FASHION

Maybe Italian men are naturally seductive. But what is certainly true is that the cut of men's clothes made in Italy – that famous relaxed chic – plays a large part in their appeal. Rome's many boutiques for men are all fairly upmarket and here you'll find a wide selection of well-cut, good quality jackets, trousers, shirts, jumpers and polo shirts, often made with finer materials and colours than their English counterparts. The Roman male has a reputation for dressing elegantly but conservatively. It's not considered good taste to stand out from the crowd, something to bear in mind if you wish to emulate the 'look'.

Emporio Armani
Via Condotti, 77 (C1)
☎ 06 321 39 92.

'What I want most is for people to express their own style through my clothes without becoming slaves to fashion.' For over 20 years, Armani has offered his contribution to fashion ideas with clothes typified by comfort and elegance in their most essential forms. Timeless, but nevertheless somehow always contemporary, his clothes really are modern classics.

Brioni
Via dei Condotti, 21 (C1)
☎ 06 678 34 28 or 06 678 36 35.

Brioni celebrated his 50th birthday by designing the 84 suits (each in 14 copies) for the Bond film, *Goldeneye*. A Brioni suit requires 18 hours of work and some 240 separate stages so these really are minor works of art. At the factory in Penne in Abruzzo, he employs 700 tailors and dressmakers and yet the 60,000 articles made every year are still not sufficient to meet demand.

Davide Cenci
Via di Campo Marzio, 1-7 (C2)
☎ 06 699 06 81.

This is where provincial members of parliament might well come to trade in their old, ill-fitting suits for some metropolitan style. For classic, smart and tasteful clothing.

Angelo Cenci
Piazza della Rotonda, 77 (C2)
☎ 06 678 14 75.

Angelo Cenci is the youngest member of the Cencis – a family that has been dressing the style-conscious Roman male for more than 60 years. The waxed cotton overcoat that's so popular nowadays costs L340,000, and a suit sells for L1,800,000. There's also a good choice of jumpers, as well as enamelled silver cufflinks.

Tombolini
Via degli Uffici del Vicario, 53 (C2)
☎ 06 678 99 41.

Here's where you'll find the simple elegance of well-cut men's clothes made from good-quality materials. There may not be many formats to choose from, but the jackets and trousers are available in three chest sizes and lengths. It's rare to come across such smart and affordable clothes in Rome.

Luigi Tella
Via Giulia, 101A (B2)
☎ 06 687 76 28.

It's impossible to have a shirt made for less than L150,000 in the centre of Rome.

And normally you'd have to wait 10 days. Here it's only two days, and, to go with the perfect shirt, you'll be given a matching tie.

Tronacarelli
Via della Cuccagna, 15
☎ 06 66 87 93 20.

This little shop was founded in 1857, and is located at the end of Piazza Navona. It's a real treasure house of hats, and a charming and welcoming place too. It sells all manner and shape of hat, for prices ranging from L80,000 to L300,000. And if it's not enough for you to leave with a real

Borsalino, you can also buy an umbrella, a scarf or a tie.

Mille Righe
Via del Gambero, 12 (C1)
☎ 06 69 92 04 50.

The list of shirts is endless – gingham, tartan, checked, emerald green, scarlet, fuchsia, cinnamon or straw-coloured, in green and blue herringbone, or with red or yellow-striped collars. So after having made your careful selection – whether single or double thread Egyptian cotton – don't forget from now on to fold back the collar and cuffs before ironing them.

Vamos per L'Uomo
Via dei Giubonnari, 102 (B3)
☎ 06 68 80 52 55.

You can kit yourself out from head to toe here, as they sell jumpers,

shirts, checked boxer shorts, and socks for the summer. And you can buy a well-cut wool or linen suit for a very reasonable price. Enough said!

Zeno
Via delle Vite, 30 (C1)
☎ 06 678 37 16.

This has the best value for money in men's ready-to-wear. Here are well-fitting, light, comfortable clothes which, if they crease, crease well. Everything is made from good fabrics – linen, cotton and velvety grey calfskin. Gabardine cotton jackets sell for L500,000, four-pocket linen and viscose jackets for L350,000, round-necked sweaters for L200,000.

NOT A SINGLE CREASE!

Don't forget to buy a 'shirt protector'. It's an Italian invention ideal in the war against creases for storing your shirts in cupboards. On sale in Spazio Sette, Via del Barbieri, it comes in two versions – a wooden one for use at home, and another, flatter, version for travelling. Very useful.

YOUNG AND BEAUTIFUL

Young Italians manage to look just as chic as their parents, though in a trendier kind of way. In Italy it's not unusual to find 25-year olds still living with their parents. Accommodation is hard to find, but with the money saved on rent, young people have more to spend on clothes. And for those who do leave the family nest, *affitti bloccati* (rents fixed at a low level) or *l'equo canone* (rents fixed at a moderate price) mean they can still have enough money to dress well – only this time mummy won't be there to do the washing and ironing.

Energie
Via del Corso, 487 (C2)
☎ 06 687 12 58.

Guaranteed good vibrations for this shop's customers as the techno music soundtrack is easily heard from the pavement. Energie sell tops, bottoms, trousers and T-shirts, all in bright colours and at unbeatable prices. They also offer a wide choice of accessories (some more wearable than others), as well as inexpensive shoes. In other words, it's the place to come to buy something in fashion without spending too much.

Josephine de Huertas
Via di Parione, 19-20 (B2)
☎ 06 68 30 01 56.

Start off, in this rather forsaken street between the Pace church and Via del Governo Vecchio, by having a look at the delightful small courtyard garden of no. 12. Then go and take a look at Josephine's clothes in this small but delightful boutique. She particularly likes working with synthetic materials such as leatherette and vinyl (trousers cost L120,000).

Onyx
Via del Corso, 132 (C1)
☎ 06 66 78 93.

Rome's youth are wild about this shop. The style plays on the theme of false innocence, though some of the clothes can still be worn even if you're over 18. The place itself is worth having a look at, with its low-key atmosphere and TV screens showing Onyx models slinking down catwalks to the accompanying sound of techno music in one part of the shop, whilst, in another, the more audacious clients try on the clothes via the interactive computer system.

Per Signorina
Via dei Giubbonari, 103 (B3).

A minuscule shop selling distinctive, good quality clothes for trendy young girls – high-cut waistcoats (L150,000), T-shirts (L45,000), mini-skirts, vinyl bags (L36,000) and stretch waxed trousers. A good place to go if you want to match a leatherette miniskirt with a pair of heavy walking boots or platform shoes.

B.B. Oil
Via dei Baullari, 129A (B2)
☎ 06 686 86 42.

Come here for a relaxed style of clothing, including sweatshirts with *Snoopy*, *Casper* and *Tiny Toons* motifs (L40,000), jeans (pre-faded if required), and lumberjack shirts. There's also a wide choice of amusing, inexpensive accessories: satchels, shoulder bags, shoes,

gloves and belts, not to mention basketball caps in team colours, lapel pins, and much more besides, all at really good prices.

Revoc
Via Lucrezio Caro, 48 (B1)
☎ 06 39 73 72 56.

Rome has many shoe shops, but few that specialise in shoes for children. That said, Revoc opts for provocation rather than more traditional designs, and few kids would ask for more than what's on offer here – all kinds of trendy boots, including Timberlands, Caterpillars ('Cats' to those in the know), and shiny shoes with buckles (L120,000) and platform soles.

Avant
Via del Corso, 170 and 171 (C1)
☎ 06 679 57 28.

Even if you think you're past the impressionable age, drop by these two shops.

HOW TO LOOK AFTER YOUR JEANS

If you don't buy them pre-washed, beware, your jeans are likely to shrink by about 10% – so buy them one size too big. Remember you can always turn up jeans that are too long, but if they're too short, you're stuck. If you buy a pair of black jeans, turn them inside out before washing them at less than 60°C/140°F, then iron them on a low heat, on a flat surface, taking care not to crease or damage the fabric. In any case, always wash them separately in the machine the first time, and never use bleach, which could ruin the fabric and discolour the jeans. If you use a dry cleaner, remember to ask for your jeans to be ironed by hand, so they don't come back as flat as a pancake which would not enable you to look very cool strolling about the Piazza di Spagna!.

One has Egyptian-theme fitting rooms, and the other is decorated in ruby reds with kitsch details and a live DJ providing a techno soundtrack. Once you've seen the decor, (avoid the crush on Saturday afternoon), have a look at the clothes. You'll often find many humorous and wearable designs, and at very reasonable prices.

SPORT AND LEISUREWEAR

Though football may be the only national sport that can empty the streets for the duration of certain televised matches, many Italians also enjoy tennis, jogging, hunting, motor or horse racing, swimming or even gymnastics. That's why you'll see many shops selling good-quality sporting outfits and accessories, often in a style reminiscent of the great American brands. As you may expect, designer labels are much in evidence, though with a hint of Italian chic.

Invicta Shop
Via del Babuino, 27 (C1)
☎ 06 36 00 17 37.

If your precious offspring seem to want to put all their worldly possessions into their bags every morning before setting off for school, then this is where you should buy them. They're all this shop sells. And you'll be surprised to find you won't need to buy them another six months later, as these bags are virtually indestructible. They come in all colours, including fluorescent ones, and every Italian teenager has one.

Dentice
Piazza Augusto Imperatore, 18-21 (C1)
☎ 06 322 60 50/06 322 60 34.

A shop for those mad about the sea, even if they only go there in their dreams. It's located at the end of Via Ripetta and sells zip-up waxed windcheaters by Ermenegildo Zegna for around L300,000, plain Superga tennis shoes for L70,000, as well as clothing in Gore-Tex and Zegna microtene – two fabrics to wear at sea if you want to be neither too hot nor too cold.

Indoni Sport
Piazza S. Vincenzo Pallotti, 208 (D2)
☎ 06 68 80 29 94.

This store actually caters for the hunting fraternity, but hunting

Italian-style means having the best gear, down to the smallest detail, windcheaters, gloves, boots – in fact everything for a solid day's hiking in the country whether or not you have your eye on a spot of game.

Linea Sport
Via del Corso, 50 (C1)
☎ 06 678 30 58.

This sports chain has several outlets in the centre of the city, so don't give up if they can't find your size – just ask directions to the next shop. And for basketball fans, there's a framed signature of Michael Jordan above the cash register.

A. Terracina
Via della Maddalena, 30A (C2)
☎ 06 686 87 37.

This shop located right by the Pantheon, is the perfect place to find leisurewear and the obligatory Superga sports shoes. With these on your feet you'll be able to perfect the Roman mid-season look you see everywhere, cotton trousers, shirt (never tucked in), or possibly T-shirt. With sunglasses worn on the crown of the head for dinner or even at the cinema, your pose will be complete regardless of the strength of the sun outside.

Palombini
Via Quattro Fontane, 107 (D2)
☎ 06 474 45 43.

Everyone knows how passionate Italians are when it comes to football and the big business that betting on matches has become. Rome has two (obviously rival) teams, Roma (1927), who play in red and yellow, and Lazio (1900),

who play in blue. This shop specialises in football kit and accessories (a pair of leather-and-synthetic goalkeeper's gloves costs around L100,000) and of course, the strips of all the Italian football teams.

Fila
Via Capo Le Case, 24 (D1)
☎ 06 678 89 73.

This is a top of the range brand very popular in the USA and has everything from T-shirts to basketball boots and sports bags. It's elegant sportswear in sober

colours, but prices are high. A sweatshirt will cost you L150,000 and 'special' basketball bags L200,000. But the quality is guaranteed.

SHOES FOR ALL FEET

It's a good time to own a shoe shop in Rome and, for once, there's as much choice for men as for women. Indeed there's something for all tastes and all pockets, whether you're looking for elegance, good leather, old-fashioned classicism, or just a chic, modern look. You can also try the food markets, where very often there will be shoe stalls around the edges, if you need to keep an eye on your expenditure.

Superattico
Via Tacito, 9 (B1)
☎ 06 323 53 81.

This minuscule shop in the Prati district is run by a very likeable couple who'll do everything to help you find exactly what you want from their selection of classic shoes. All are made from surprisingly supple leather, and retail at moderate prices (around L100,000).

Impronta
Via del Governo Vecchio, 1 (B2)
☎ 06 689 69 47.

The Via del Governo Vecchio is acquiring a growing reputation for fashion. Impronta is keeping up with the latest trends by offering shoes made by some of the capital's best designers. A pair of sandals or unfussily elegant shoes will cost L150,000-L200,000.

Borini
Via dei Pettinari, 86-87 (B3)
☎ 06 687 56 70.

Though you may not be impressed by the appearance of this shop, and its assistants are not always very welcoming, Romans fight over the latest arrivals at the start of each season. You'll find examples of the latest fashions on display, but also some updated classics, all made from such supple leather that polishing your shoes will be a pleasure (prices L100,000-200,000).

Alberto
Piazza B. Cairoli, 13-15 (C3)
☎ 06 686 11 88.

Do yourself a favour and visit this shop which is always busy. You're bound to find exactly what you want from the hundreds of models displayed in the window (point them out and give your size). Leather moccasins or sandals for L40,000. A good place to go if your pockets are feeling much lighter than they were at the start of your stay.

Adriana Campanile
Piazza di Spagna, 88 (C1)
☎ 06 69 92 23 55.

This new designer knows how to wed fashion and tradition in the most elegant ways. It's the best place to go for a good deal as it's a discount store and since it's right in the historic centre, it's easy to find. Adriana Campanile hasn't forgotten your children's little feet either – so you can kill two birds with one stone. Average price L150,000.

Coggi
Via G.C. Belli, 81 (B1)
☎ 06 320 19 57.

This shop in the Prati district sells handmade shoes for women only. You can select the style and heel height, as well as the type of leather or other material you require.

Bruno Magli
Via del Gambero, 1 (C1)
☎ 06 679 38 02.

Choose this label (originally from Bologna) and you can't go wrong. Magli certainly knows how to combine old and new by adding a modern touch to his classic designs and making them appear less conservative. A pair of elegant shoes with medium heels sells for L150,000. There's an ample range of new designs to choose from, as well as many updated classics. Magli is famous for loafers.

Barillà
Via Condotti, 29 (C1)
Via Belsiana, 44 (C1)
Via del Babuino, 33A (C1)
and Via del Leone, 17 (C1)
☎ 06 66 87 10 09.

This chain produces classic (but not too sober) shoes, as well as a few trendier items in every new collection. Prices are reasonable (about L100,000). It's also worth knowing that if they don't have your size (*misura*) they'll phone

Brugnoli
Via del Babuino,
57 (C1)
☎ 06 36 00 19 16.

With its high ceilings, leather armchairs, and all the attention lavished on details, this shop is more like a large lounge, where it's a pleasure to take the weight off your feet and remove your shoes. The very competent assistants will help you choose from the huge range available.

around the other shops and a runner will bring them to you in less than 10 minutes.

Follie
Via Bellinzona, 11.

This is a shop far from the city centre that makes handmade shoes for men and women. Though you need wait no more than two days, prices are high.

PERCHING ON HIGH HEELS

Is the frequent wearing of high heels bad for your health? Probably, yes. Much has been said about the negative effects on the spinal column of the distribution of the weight of the body over only a small surface area. Here's a little physics for you: a woman weighing 60kg/132lb wearing high heels exerts a weight of 90-150kg/198-330lb over a heel area of $2.5cm^2/1in^2$ at every step.

KNITWEAR, SWEATERS AND WOOLLENS

It's difficult to talk about Italian fashion without mentioning knitwear and woollens. Though you may already know Missoni and his varied and colourful creations, in Rome you'll discover designers who work as craftsmen creating one-offs, which unfortunately are never cheap, but it's fun to look nevertheless. But there are brands that cost less and could keep you equally warm next winter.

Solo Cashmere made in Italy
Via del Babuino, 105A (C1)
☎ 06 679 84 88.

Unlike English cashmere designs (which are usually classic though sometimes considered a little old-fashioned), those on display here (for both men and women) are elegantly-cut and in fashionable colours. However, the prices are high.

Bomba
Via dell'Oca, 39 (C1)
☎ 06 320 30 20.

For over 30 years now, this has been the best place for original and stylish woollens and jumpers. Everything is made using traditional methods, and the owner, Cristina, herself a designer, will help you make your choice.

Balloon
Largo del Pallaro, 19 (B3)
and Piazza di Spagna, 35 (C1)
☎ 06 678 01 10/
06 678 98 06.

This is very popular with Romans and you'll find perfectly-cut clothes, in classic colours, including light, close-fitting jumpers to be worn with a lady's suit, or looser jumpers to go with trousers, as well as men's or women's silk or mixed silk-cashmere pyjamas for L80,000. The style is close to that of the French designer Agnès B. Generally not too expensive.

Leclercq
Via delle Carrozze, 50 (C1)
☎ 06 687 49 45.

Diana, who wanted to become a painter, takes great care choosing the colours for her designs, sometimes as many as 35 in a

single jumper. Her unique knitwear is all hand-made, which accounts for the high prices – some of the more expensive items sell for about a million lire. The actor John Malkovich is one of the Leclercq sisters' famous clients.

WATCH WHERE YOU'RE PUTTING YOUR FEET!

Italian shoe sizes differ from those you are used to (see p.126 for more information), and shoe and sock sizes do not correspond in Italy:

SHOES	35	36	37	38	39/40	41	42	43	44	45
SOCKS	8	8.5	9	9.5	10	10.5	11	11.5	12	12.5

Wladimir
Via della Vite, 21 (C1)
☎ 06 322 09 37.

This is not the place to look for a plain, good-quality sweater. Although the prices are indeed reasonable, these sweaters (for both men and women) come in vivid colours with imaginative little touches, such as small knitted collars. You'll pay L90,000 for a round-collared Fair Isle jumper.

Cashemere e Cashemere
Via Ripetta, 69 (C1)
☎ 06 321 05 99.

This is a place where visitors and Romans alike, tired from a busy day, can relax a little and admire the classic and elegant designs in this shop. A hushed atmosphere reigns and white is very much the dominant colour together with many creamy variations. Expect to pay around L400,000 for a jumper.

Barbara Gregori
Via Vittoria, 37 (C1)
☎ 06 33 21 18 18.

Near Piazza del Popolo, this small shop is very popular with Romans, who come here to buy very good quality jumpers, as well as ladies' wool suits (L600-800,000) and elegant blouses.

Tiziana Modiano
Via Belsiana, 11 (C1)
☎ 06 679 37 59.

In the old-fashioned atmosphere of this shop, with its light wooden display shelves and red hexagonal floor tiles, you'll find attractive jumpers in pastel shades that you'll have no trouble wearing with a skirt or trousers. Prices around L200,000-L300,000.

ITALY SOCKS IT TO THE WORLD

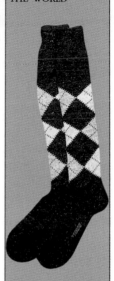

Italy ranks at the forefront of world sock production and regularly sells something in the region of 750 million pairs a year. There is even a sock museum in Milan, where you can learn, for example, that the most elegant socks are long socks, and that Khruschev wore his too short. Some people, like Jacques Chirac and Silvio Berlusconi, like them black, others, of course, prefer them red, like Italy's (now dead) writer Alberto Moravia.

Penelope
Via Belsiana, 5 (C1).

Yet more jumpers, this time in classic or more modern styles. You'll find a wide choice of colours all at attractively affordable prices. This a very popular shop with the Romans and well worth a visit.

LINGERIE, CHIC AND SEXY

Italians are real professionals when it comes to chic and sexy underwear. For ladies' lingerie try Malizia, Christies, Occhi Verdi and Eurocorset, and for men Versace and Dolce & Gabbana. Philippe Matignon, New York, Ori and Pierre Mantoux, are excellent for tights and stockings. Kristina T. and Chiaruggi sell colourful swimsuits. Sensual delight and comfort are guaranteed, with labels such as Ragno and Boglietti. By the way, the Italian for lingerie is *biancheria intima*.

La Perla
Via Condotti, 78 (C1)
☎ 06 678 08 33.

This prestigious name in luxury ladies' underwear famed for its elegance, simplicity and fine fabrics, such as silk and satin, has now also brought out negligées for nights of romance. Very much as you'd expect to find in a shop selling such luxurious items, the decor is understated in pale woods with goods displayed on simple racks. It's expensive (a silk and lace bra is L550,000), but when you're in love…

Intimo 3
Via Campo Marzio, 45 (C2), Via dei Due Macelli, 67 (D1).

This Italian chain is for people who prefer another type of underwear, no frills, and in cotton or a coarser material, but always simple. For men, there are also pyjamas and bathrobes.

Il Fiocco
Via del Gambero, 13 (C1)
☎ 06 679 06 19.

Red underwear is neither vulgar nor provocative and in Italy, red is considered a lucky colour on 1st January. Whether superstitious or not, everyone wears red underwear on the first day of the year, just in case it does bring prosperity. So if you find yourself wandering through

Italian streets towards the end of the year, don't be surprised to see the displays in lingerie shops have turned bright red. Seize the opportunity and go for red!

lace decoration. The choice is wide and prices fairly high. In the spring, they have all the latest swimwear. This is the place to come before heading for the coast's more fashionable beaches.

Demoiselle
Via Frattina, 93 (C1)
☎ 06 679 37 52.

Despite offering a wide choice, this shop offers no real challenge to its nearest rival, Vanità. Here the displays are kept simple, and items range from cotton sports underwear (L30,000) to silk underwear for ladies who want elegance and refinement (L230,000). A nice selection at reasonable prices.

Tebro
Via dei Prefetti, 46 (C2)
☎ 06 687 34 41.

Romans have always known this shop, which has kept its timeless appearance and offers a wide choice of plain, comfortable and classic garments (for both men and women) – attractive striped cotton boxer shorts (L16,000) to go with shirts, traditional underpants by *La Perla Uomo*, breezy nightgowns, and loose cotton tops for lazy lie-ins.

Vanità
Via Frattina, 25 (C1)
☎ 06 679 17 43.

This small shop is one of the best addresses for lingerie – where numerous stars come to buy delicate, hand-embroidered lingerie with delightful

DE RITIS

Via Santa Chiara, 38 (C2)
☎ 06 686 58 43.

Here in a vast shop near the Pantheon you can indulge your religious side. They have bed jackets for nuns, viscose tunics for novices, purple socks for cardinals, warm dressing gowns for monks who suffer the cold, and slippers for mother superiors, i.e. everything the clergy could possibly want. And while the window display may not be very exciting and the sales assistants certainly behind the fashion times, it's the perfect place to buy a warm and comfortable present for an elderly relative who feels the cold. So make sure you stock up for winter.

Simona
Via del Corso, 83 (C1)
☎ 06 36 00 18 36.

The bra may have gone out of fashion during the 1920s and again during the 1970s, but today the Italian equivalent of the wonderbra is all the rage (around L70,000). And here in this shop, panty fetishists, stocking and suspender lovers and collectors of corsets will be able to give free reign to their imaginations. Admittedly, some of the range isn't in the best of taste, but makes an interesting display nonetheless.

FINE LEATHER GOODS

Good quality Italian leather is not only used to make shoes. People with a taste for elegance also require bags, belts, gloves, wallets, not to mention items for the office and other accessories. The hallmarks of the Italian leather trade are its long tradition of craftsmanship and a dedication to the object produced no matter what its size.

Gucci
Via Condotti, 8 (C1)
☎ 06 678 93 40.

The famous 'bamboo' bag was, as you may already know, designed by Gucci, probably Rome's foremost fine leather craftsman. For some time now, a young American designer, Tom Ford, has been helping Gucci's venerable fashion house to revitalise its style, which is just as famous for silk headscarves and ties, with some success, as the company is now listed on the Milan Stock Exchange.

Le Sac
Via della Vite, 44/45 (C1)
☎ 06 679 45 97.

You may be taken aback by the abundance of it all. The window displays are so packed – with bags for both men and women, wallets, key-rings, office accessories, etc. – that you won't know where to look. All the goods are highly attractive and even affordable. A good place to come to buy a typically Italian gift without spending the earth.

Ceintures
Via dei Giubbonari, 60 (B3).

This shop only sells leather belts for men. They're available in hide, imitation crocodile and braided leather, in all colours and sizes, and with various metal adornments. For the trendier among you, there's also chain belts.

Furla
Via Cola di Rienzo, 226-228 (B1), Via Tomacelli, 136 (C1)
☎ 06 687 45 05.

Currently one of the most popular brands. Every season, Furla brings out the most audacious designs for bags. You may be also enticed by the wallets, which are all equally attractive, or the costume jewellery.

Sermoneta
Piazza di Spagna, 61 (C1)
☎ 06 679 19 60.

You'll find a wide selection of gloves at this shop. And here's an important piece of advice, your white hide gloves should be washed with milk and liquid soap, but for leathers and kid which should never be washed,

gossip on the pretext of looking for a pair of smart gloves.

Santini
Via Frattina, 120 (C1)
☎ 06 678 41 14.

The boutique is decorated 1970s-style with large white cubes, on

which are displayed designer bags for trendy young things. Take a look at the rucksacks, the very original wallets and the covers for laptop computers. Good for modern leather goods, and a variety of unusual gifts.

Coccinelle
Via Cola di Rienzo, 225 (B1)
☎ 06 324 17 49.

This is Furla's major rival, and here you'll find all the most

spot clean with petrol, in moderation. Gloves are generally good value for money in Rome, and coupled with the fact that they take up almost no extra room in your suitcase, they're a very good present to take home with you.

D'Auria
Via Due Macelli, 55 (D1)
☎ 06 679 33 64.

This family of glovers, once suppliers to the king himself, has had a shop since 1885. The decor is elegant, turn of the century with imposing chandeliers, cane armchairs, and wallpaper the colour of champagne. It's not surprising, then, that ladies would come here for a chat and a bit of

up to date creations, made from good quality leather at fairly reasonable prices. Another good place for buying gifts for friends or treating yourself.

Mandarina Duck
Via Cola di Rienzo, 270-272 (B1), Corso Vittore Emanuele II, 16 (B2)
☎ 06 66 89 64 91.

The label Italians were wild about a dozen years ago has updated itself. As well as bags in light synthetic material, they now sell colourful leather bags, rucksacks and small leather articles. Prices are sometimes a little on the high side.

INTERIOR DECORATION

It's worth making the detour just to see the showrooms displaying interior decoration items especially since they are often housed in beautiful settings such as lofts and palazzi with ornamental ceilings. Objects are displayed with great finesse for the appreciation of all Italians, who are usually most attentive to the insides of their homes, in marked contrast to the often charmingly dilapidated exteriors.

Beatrice Palma
Via dei Pianellari, 17 (B2)
☎ 06 686 12 63
Closed Sat. afternoon.

On display in the window are replicas of ancient medallions delicately set against ivory drapes. Inside you'll find inexpensive, unusual souvenirs, including

well-finished, life size or miniature plaster or clay busts, and many other architectural fragments – scallops, acanthus leaves, angels, wreathed columns, plump cherubs, capitals, hands and feet – all displayed in studied disorder.

Magazzini Formae Memoria
P. della Rovere, 107 (A2)
☎ 06 683 29 15.

This showroom is housed over three floors of an ex-printing

works overlooking the Tiber. Here the architect, Pino Pasquali, sells his latest creations, such as the *Dott. Curzio* desk (three million lire), as well as bathroom accessories and oak furniture for children's rooms. You'll find heavy

discounts in the sales held twice a year.

Alivar
Piazza Campitelli, 2 (C3)
☎ 06 679 69 74.

If you're on the lookout for perfect copies of the 'classics' of contemporary furniture (by Alvar Aalto, MacKintosh and Le Corbusier), this is the place to come. You'll also find more recent pieces, such as the S-Chair by Cappellini (L200,000).

Fontana Arte
Vicolo Sugarelli, 12 (B2)
☎ 06 686 41 48.

Fontana Arte are specialists in light fittings. They sell recent works by Philippe Starck such as the Romeo Moon lamp (L590,000) which uses the transparency of glass for its visual effect. Another Starck creation is the Ara table lamp in chrome-plated metal (L495,000) that lights up according to the way it's facing.

Farnese
Piazza Farnese, 52 (B3)
☎ 06 689 61 09.

This is Rome's most beautiful shop and showroom specialising in tiles, an art form that started in the 15th century. Ferous oxide mixed with Tuscan clays produces a bright red, and mixed with Umbran clay gives more delicate

just as easily have an up-to-date look as a Rococo style, but always with a touch of humour.

'L'Ambiance' Sermonetta
Via del Babuino, 130 (C1)
☎ 06 679 06 81.

This shop specialises in embroidered curtains (L35-60,000) with a Tyrolean motif (thistles and edelweisses on red, white and green backgrounds), but also carries out commissions. The perfect place to shop if you want to make sure your tablecloths and curtains don't clash, or you want to make the inside of your house look like something out of *Heidi*. There's also a good choice of regional furniture painted with trompe-l'oeil designs.

tones of yellow, pink and gold. The whole place is more like a museum, with marble tables in the antique style, mosaics, and a mixture of Roman, Pompeian and Baroque art. At prices as sumptuous as the creations.

Artemua
Via dei Barbieri, 29 (C3)
☎ 06 66 87 72 64.

Light-fitters play an important part in the creation of Italian interior design and here we have a specialist. He uses cast iron and glass to create lamps that could

Soleiado di Sanda
Via dell'Oca, 38A (C1)
☎ 06 361 04 02.

This shop in a small street near Piazza del Popolo overflows with splendid fabrics from Northern Italy. It also sells chairs, stools, candlesticks and crockery in colours from Lombardy, Veneto and Piedmont. All objects that will give your home a warm and typically Italian touch.

Naka
Via del Corso, 149 (C1)
☎ 06 679 19 96.

A fairly touristy shop selling numerous small objects for the table – pepper pots (around L100,000), cutlery, candlesticks and traditional plates. It's an elegant selection with Southern designs. Have a look at the trompe-l'oeil plates (decorated with fruit, vegetables and fish).

GIFTS AND SOUVENIRS

Rome offers all kinds of choice and prices for everything, from standard souvenirs to more unusual presents. From the cheapest T-shirts to the most expensive antiques, you'll enjoy wandering through its maze of small streets until you spot the ideal gift.

Cecconi
Via del Pellegrino, 95 (B2)
☎ 06 68 80 65 77.

This goldsmith is expert at copying old jewellery. Amongst other typically Italian items are silver votives which are used as religious offerings. You can have these engraved and there are a variety of designs to choose from – each moulded from a slender sheet of silver.

Deletré
Via Fontanella Borghese, 3 (C1)
☎ 06 687 77 22.

Karl Lagerfeld designed the logo for this innovative costume jewellery shop. Inside, rock crystal and semi-precious stones from Sri Lanka and Brazil are shown at their best in audacious Art Nouveau-style settings. Suffice it to say, Deletré is a firm favourite among the rich and famous. A sapphire and emerald bracelet will cost around L200,000.

Nardecchia
Piazza Navona, 25 (B2)
☎ 06 656 93 18.

If you appreciate quaint water-colours of Vesuvius erupting, or the romantic depictions of ancient ruins that Labruzzi (1748-1817) did for those embarked on the 'Grand Tour', then you'll find what you're looking for here. There's a fine collection of 17th to 19th-century prints with which you can amuse yourself recognising views of Rome before the excavation of the Roman Forum. Nardecchia also has scenes of daily life in the 18th century painted by Pinelli. Prices range from L300,000 to three million lire.

Cereria Pisoni
Via dei Giubbonari, 96 (B3)
☎ 06 66 86 16 05.

This shop selling handmade candles in the heart of the historic city centre has been here since 1803. The candles are sold in the shape of churches, among other unusual forms, both perfumed and unperfumed.

Now there's an idea for a cheap and original present!

Acanto
Via della Stelletta, 10 (C2)
☎ 06 686 54 81.

You should be able to find some small item at a reasonable price (haggling is mandatory) to satisfy your need for a piece of the past. On sale are charming silver trinkets, excellent copies of Baroque gilt picture frames in all sizes (L100,000), and cheap curios hidden away amidst all the confusion. A great place to hunt around without spending a fortune and from which to bring back a genuine Roman souvenir. It may also give you plenty of ideas for decoration.

Hollywood
Via Monserrato, 107 (B2)
☎ 06 686 91 97.

If you haven't had time to go and visit the former film studios in Cinecittà, you might want to drop by this shop which is a treasure trove for film buffs. You'll be able to pick up posters (*locandine*) from the good old days of Italian cinema, as well as many other souvenirs. It's a good place for videos too.
Well worth a visit if you are a cinema-goer interested in the history of Italian films.

Franzini bric-a-brac
Via Brunetti, 40 (C1)
☎ 06 361 03 09.

Collectors will find all kinds of things of interest in this treasure trove: salt cellars, perfume-burners, silver objects and old prints (framed and unframed), as well as religious souvenirs. With no more than L50,000 you'll be able to return home with something lovely and original that you couldn't find anywhere outside the Eternal City.

Gini O. Graphics
Piazza della Chiesa Nuova, 21 (B2),
Via Nazionale, 185 (D2)
☎ 06 686 46 47.

This is the home of the Roman souvenir – sold in every imaginable shape, size and form, from T-shirts to mugs and wristwatches. So it's a good place to come to if you're looking for somewhere interesting to shop for last minute gifts on a Sunday afternoon when your plane doesn't leave until the evening.

Vertecchi
Via della Croce, 38 and 70 (C1)
☎ 06 66 79 01 55.

This is much more than just a stationery shop. It's full of all kinds of other colourful and original articles. On one side of the street they sell satchels, designer bags and posters, and on the other you can hunt through a range of pens, calendars and Italian diaries. If you follow the markings on the floor you'll find your way into the annexe, which specialises in party decorations and accessories. It's an opportunity to bring back all you need to decorate a Christmas tree Italian-style or to try some of the very ornate Italian Easter eggs.

Push
Corso Vittorio Emanuele II, 37A (B2)
☎ 06 66 79 71 54.

This is a useful place to go to stock up on some new T-shirts. And with prices starting at L5,000, you've really got no excuse not to bring back something for everyone.

FOR THE VERY YOUNG

Italians absolutely adore children and allow them into virtually any establishment. However, oddly enough, more and more Italians are choosing to have only one child which they make the absolute centre of attention. It follows that in Rome you'll be spoilt for choice and are bound to find something to dress up or amuse your own offspring.

La Città del Sole
Via della Scrofa, 65 (C2)
☎ 06 687 54 04.

Here you'll find toys, but also good games – model kits for budding archeologists, jigsaws of Roman mosaics, cardboard kits of the Colosseum and other Roman monuments, like the pretty Tempietto di San Pietro (see p.65). One of many ways to satisfy the young and bring back a piece of the Eternal City.

La Cigogna
Via Cola di Rienzo, 268 (A1),
Via Frattina, 138 (C1)
☎ 06 698 65 57/
06 679 19 12.

As almost everyone knows, children are brought to earth by storks. Hence the name of this chain of shops, where you'll find everything for young children, as well as future mums, to wear. Apart from the christening clothes and smart outfits for the very young (such as only the Italians still know how to make) you'll also find some very nice leisurewear (to age 14).

Il Bauletto
Via della Farnesina, 11 (B3)
☎ 06 334 08 42.

These inexpensive secondhand clothes for children (0-12) have all been properly

sterilised and are totally hygenic. You have two choices – either a swap, if you're bringing in clothes, or a purchase if you're coming empty-handed.
A good system for parents a little short of money.

Al Sogno
Piazza Navona, 53 (B2)
☎ 06 66 86 41 98.

This is Rome's most unbelievable toy shop, and probably its most expensive. It specialises in cuddly toys for all tastes and at all prices. They range from the miniature tortoise to the life-size black panther (which could set you back L610,000). They also have one of Italy's more famous fictional characters for children – Pinocchio.

Biancaneve e i sette nani
Via Metastasio, 17 (C2)
☎ 06 686 54 09.

This hairdresser is an unusual place specially created for children. Instead of chairs, they provide painted wooden horses, which fascinate the children and allow the very patient hairdressers to get on with their job with minimum interruption.

Bidonville
Via dei Volsci, 5 (not on map).

This new shop in the San Lorenzo district is worth a detour, despite the name (which means 'shanty town'). It's a strange place selling toys, books, records, and clothes for both children and adults. You have two choices, either you accept a swap, e.g. bring two records and leave with one (valid on all products), or you buy something outright knowing that nothing will cost more than L30,000.

Iana
Via Cola di Rienzo, 182 (B1)
☎ 06 68 89 26 68.

This unassuming shop is perhaps one of the best places for finding a really Roman gift for your best friend's baby. The items are pretty, imaginative, tasteful, colourful and, what's more, attractive and quite affordable.

METTIMI GIU
Via due Macelli, 59A (D1)
☎ 06 66 78 97 61.

This shop sells clothes for children up to the age of 15. The clothes are brightly coloured and quite the opposite of classic children's clothes. Unfortunately, despite being attractive, the prices are a little high.

FOR THE HOME

Here you'll find a wide choice of traditional products – terracotta tiles, smart household linens and other useful or decorative items. You'll easily come to the conclusion that Italians have a natural sense of style when it comes to interior decoration.

Cucina
Via del Babuino, 118 (C1)
☎ 06 684 08 19.

Traditional objects are on sale here in a hi-tech basement. The star of the show is the 'bottle-measure' for wine. Designed in the 15th century, it has on its neck an official lead stamp melded into the glass: *fojetta* is equivalent to a half-litre, and the *barzilai*, two litres, takes its name from a member of parliament who used to give it as a 'present' to any potential voter (around L20,000).

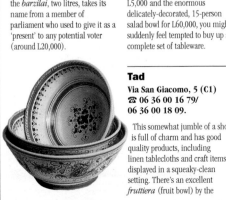

Marini e Poli
Via del Pellegrino, 85 (B2)
☎ 06 686 96 98.

There are few shops like this in the heart of the historic city centre. It's more of an Ali Baba's cave spilling out onto the pavement. Have a good look round for hand-made ceramics at unbeatable prices and when you've seen the pencil pot for L5,000 and the enormous delicately-decorated, 15-person salad bowl for L60,000, you might suddenly feel tempted to buy up a complete set of tableware.

Tad
Via San Giacomo, 5 (C1)
☎ 06 36 00 16 79/
06 36 00 18 09.

This somewhat jumble of a shop is full of charm and has good quality products, including linen tablecloths and craft items displayed in a squeaky-clean setting. There's an excellent *fruttiera* (fruit bowl) by the

designer Achille Castiglioni with drainer incorporated so that you can place fruit that has just been rinsed on the table (L200,000).

Paolo Agostara
Via di Santa Chiara, 8 (C2)
☎ 06 689 37 77.

You might make a lucky find in this long narrow shop, which has

many tastefully-chosen items from all over the world – wire candlesticks (L50,000) and

teapots in the shape of cats (L40,000), as well as cat-motif doormats, ashtrays and plates.

BBK
Via della Frezza, 60 (C1)
☎ 06 324 36 88/
06 324 42 59.

Short for Bed, Bath and Kitchen, (trendy for Italians!), BBK is a refined and eclectic shop, and one which manages to combine the latest style with a certain chic. There's a good range of objects for the home, with many natural materials. The glassware is attractive and admirably displayed. And you'll also find examples of Italian design.

Frette
Piazza di Spagna, 10 (C1)
☎ 06 679 06 73.

This shop already has a well-established reputation. The bed linen comes in natural and unbleached colours and the latest collections are usually displayed on an enormous bed. A sheet will cost around L300,000.

In Folio
Corso Vittorio Emanuele II, 261-263 (B2)
☎ 06 66 86 14 46.

This shop in the historic centre sells all the sleekest modern design articles Italy has to offer. Apart from the latest in coffeepots or transparent, originally-shaped vases, it also has a beautiful collection of pens and watches.

Bassetti
Via del Teatro Valle, 15 (C2)
☎ 06 698 28 78.

This famous name in bathroom linen sells discounted end-of-collections (*scampoli*) that could make you forget the new ones. Have a look at their bath towels amusingly printed with famous paintings.

TERRACOTTA

This art form dates back to the 15th century and nowadays is still used most for bowls, tiles, garden containers and slates. In Italy there are two discernible styles, in Tuscany, Impruneta is famous for its red pottery, which contains ferrous oxide in the clay, whilst in Umbria, terracotta is a yellowish-pink or gold. Common decorative motifs for terracotta are interlacing acanthus leaves, baskets of fruit, seashells, singing cherubs, angels and eagles.

Tupini
Piazza in Lucina, 8 (C1)
☎ 06 687 14 58.

This is a lovely shop decorated with displays of porcelain and china plates and examples of Murano glass. If you're on honeymoon, it might be the place to make up any oversights in your wedding list. It's as much a small museum as a shop.

SECONDHAND CLOTHES

The craze for buying secondhand clothes started a dozen or so years ago when the Japanese started buying up (without quibbling over prices) stocks of old American jeans, so now 1960s and 1970s jeans made with an indigo material weighing up to 400gm (14oz) are in great demand. But what's even more sought-after is 'dead stock', i.e. old clothes that have never been worn. Polo-neck jumpers, Paco Rabane-style, are also highly prized. In other words, old is cool.

L'Usato
Piazza Campo dei Fiori, 14 (B3).

This shop stocks all three of the legendary American brands, namely Levi's, Lee and Wrangler. As collectors will know, Levi jeans made before 1966 have a capital E on the small brand label and the old-style jackets have an extra fold in the front and an adjustable belt at the back. So-called 'first generation' Wranglers have a single breast pocket, the 'second generation' have two.

Seconda Mano
Via del Governo Vecchio, 85 (B2)
☎ 06 687 99 95.

This is the smartest of the second-hand clothes shops. A sewing machine in the corner tells you that the clothes here are often altered, probably essential to give them a more contemporary look.

Seconda Mano
Via della Lungara, 42 (B3).

Despite having the same name, this shop (close to the Regina Coeli prison) has a totally different atmosphere. It sells all sorts, genuine and false Lacostes, stripy shirts, polo shirts with no label, baggy shirts with two patch pockets, collarless shirts (usually bought by women), and more.

Stalls on Piazza del Paradiso

The stalls are open at irregular intervals and the quality on offer can vary. Nor is it really 'paradise', but, if you're very lucky, you might find the legendary 'one-O-one', the famous 1931 Lee jacket

GREEN IS GOOD!

According to the director of a recycling company the process of recycling clothes is not wearing thin:

'*For every ton of clothes we receive, a third is wearable, another third is reusable as industrial cleaning cloth, and the last third, depending on the composition of the material, finds its way into the sweaters of well-known manufacturers whose labels state '100% wool'. And finally, any remnants go to the cardboard industry or to be destroyed.*'

with two breast pockets and zigzag stitching on the flap. A great place for all would-be James Deans.

Mille Vite
Via della Chiesa Nuova, 17 (B2)
☎ 06 68 80 38 90.

This shop specialises in 1960s garb, so you'll see a lot of orange (the in-colour of the time), as well as bell-bottoms and heaps of fake Paco Rabanne polo necks. They also sell plenty of multicoloured and translucent accessories to go with the sunglasses on sale for less than L15,000.

Paola
Via Corsini, 69 (B3)
☎ 06 589 53 60.

This very upper middle-class Roman lady sees by appointment (in Trastevere) equally upper middle-class clients who are looking for secondhand designer clothes. For L200,000, for example, she'll find you a very nice Valentino jacket.

Sempre Verde
Via del Governo Vecchio, 26 (B2)
☎ 06 68 80 13 96.

Maybe you've come to the wrong

place – the window's cracked, the door broken and the dummies have their heads covered in sheets of newspaper. But it's all part of the intended effect in this 'shabby-chic' shop. And you'll be surprised to find the clothes are very wearable.

NOT FORGETTING...

Sophia Luciani
Via Sicilia, 154 ☎ 06 487 35 56
By appointment only.
Very affordable prices.

Il Mercatino
Via L. Respighi, 16
☎ 06 807 98 55 or 06 687 20 49
Secondhand luxury children's clothes. Even Armani.

Discount Alta Moda
Via Gesu e Maria, 16
☎ 06 361 37 97
Bags by Gucci and Chanel, as well as a new designer, Venturi, who is much appreciated by all fashionable Roman ladies.

Discount delle Firme
Via Serviti, 27 ☎ 06 482 77 90
Sells previous years' collections at 50%.

Discount System
Via Viriniale, 35 ☎ 06 474 65 45
Luxury bargains.

Abiti Usati
Via del Governo Vecchio, 35 (B2).

This is the queen of all the secondhand clothes shops. Among the mountains of clothes from all eras and who knows where, you might find, if you've time, the perfect 1960s mini-skirt, but be prepared to rummage.

Mado
Via del Governo Vecchio, 89A (B2).

This is the place to come to find out about fashion in the 1930s. With a cosy bygone decor, this shop sells the clothes and accessories that today's Italian grandmothers might have worn.

ANTIQUES

Collectors, professional or amateur, should be able to pick up much of interest in Rome's secondhand and antique shops (some truly excellent), or in art galleries, or in the famous Trastevere flea market. But real bargains are hard to come by. A word of warning – crowded open-air markets are ideal hunting grounds for nimble-fingered pickpockets, so be careful and good luck with that find of the century.

Mercantino dei Partigiani

Piazzale dei Partigiani (not on the map) 1st Sun. of the month, except Aug.

This small flea market is held in the basement of a garage and sells furniture and objects from the 1940s and 1950s. Sometimes you even see middle-class housewives from smart districts selling family items. The prices are really low, so that for L30,000 you can pick up a 1950s yellow and pink formica table, a style Italians refer to as *modernariato*.

Porta Portese

Sun. 6.30am-2pm (not on the map).

This is the main flea market held at the back of Trastevere. Here you'll find a bit of everything (including the occasional stolen item), though ultimately it's disappointing if you're on the lookout for a real bargain. They also have a lot of new goods for sale – jeans and leather jackets made in Korea (L200,000), and terracotta copies of antique decoration and the occasional oil lamp. Of course, you should haggle, if only for the pleasure (watch out for pickpockets!).

Underground

Via Crispi, 96 (D1) ☎ 06 69 94 04 40

2nd Sat. and Sun. of the month; entrance L3,000. This is a relatively new flea market that is held in a huge 4-floor garage between Piazza del Popolo and Via Veneto. There's a bit of everything here, including a certain Mario Ambrosini, a screenwriter who worked with Fellini, who sells the miniature gifts you find in Kinder chocolate eggs to collectors and members of the Kindermania club. Prices vary and are often on the high side.

Dal Papa Re
Via P. Castaldi, 16-18 (not on the map)
☎ 06 588 31 38.

Located in the centre of Trastevere is this strangely-named cavern of 18th and 19th-century antiques. It's open on Sunday mornings, and is the place for dedicated amateurs who are searching for that rare object at an unbeatable price.

Marmistica Bonuccelli
Via dei Coronari, 200 (B2)
☎ 06 687 99 27.

This clever craftsman makes low tables in various sizes (for a million lire) using leftovers of ancient marble, and turns various architectural fragments into shelves and picture frames. Your visit will also be the opportunity for you to become more familiar with *intarsia*, i.e. stone marquetry, which was a popular luxury in ancient times. Anything you request can be commissioned.

Altogether a refined and typically Roman place, which can also deliver abroad.

Mario Prili
Via dei Banchi Nuovi, 47 (B2)
☎ 06 68 80 60 52.

In 1966, Sor Mario, the owner of this shop, received a special award for having found a Botticelli stolen in 1820 from a Roman art collector. Indeed, he has a real flair for buying up really fine goods from aristocratic families fallen on hard times that he quickly sells on at good prices. The shop, guaranteed to have a

few surprises in store, is something of a mess, but all the more charming for it. Go along for yourselves, there's always something of interest on offer. Haggling is obligatory and Sor Mario is something else.

TANCA ANTIQUES
S. dei Crescenzi, 12 (C2)
☎ 06 68 80 60 52.

In an alleyway leading onto the Pantheon, hidden away over several floors, you'll find this dealer who has, amongst many other treasures (icons, silverware, watercolours, cameos and rare objects), an impressive collection of Borbonici earrings (19th-century) originating from the states once under the rule of the Bourbons (i.e. Naples and southern Italy). A unique collection.

Carlo Virgilio
Via dell Lupa, 10 (C2)
☎ 06 687 10 93.

This art gallery sells 19th and 20th-century drawings at very reasonable prices (from L300,000 to rarely more than a million lire).They have a good selection of views of Rome and its surroundings from bygone eras, which can make charming and original souvenirs. This is a place well-known to collectors and curators, and in Carlo Virgilio's catalogue a few years ago, there was even a drawing by the visionary early 20th-century French architect, Lequeu.

FOOD AND WINE

Shopping for food in Italy can be like entering a time warp. Assistants in the *salsamenterie* (grocer's) still wear white overalls and scribble the bill with the stub of pencil tucked behind their ears. Because supermarkets in Rome are relegated to the outskirts of the town, Roman grocery stores still sell everything – from bread to tinned goods and washing powder. And here you'll run into real Romans going about their daily life.

Pasta all'uovo
Via della Croce, 8 (C1).

A window display worthy of Italian painter Arcimboldo, consisting of all colours and all kinds of pasta. Customers crowd the counter at this popular shop and it's no surprise to learn that it specialises in fresh pasta. You'll find all sorts including spaghetti, tagliatelle, penne rigate and ravioli (with various fillings). Fresh pasta can easily be kept for 10 days, though ravioli, the most delicate, for only three or four.

Ruggeri
Via della Pace, 29 (B2)
☎ 06 680 14 24.

This unassuming shop right behind the Pace market sells a good selection of olive oils, *De Cecco* (L13,000), *Sasso* (L11,000) and *Monini* (L10,000). They also have olive oils from Sicily and Southern Italy, but remember, airlines consider olive oil to be a combustible substance and so ration the amount you can transport. You'll also find *Sambuca*, a sweet aniseed Roman liqueur that's drunk with a coffee bean floating on the surface or with ice.

Nanni
Via della Croce, 25 (C1)
☎ 06 679 17 69.

All the local celebrities come here to fight over the latest delivery of *bottarga* (dried cod eggs to be grated over pasta) from Sardinia. You can also buy vacuum-packed parmesan, which won't take up much space in your luggage.

Buccone
Via di Ripetta, 19 (C1)
☎ 06 361 21 54.

The period decor here puts you in mind of a neo-medieval castle built in the 1930s. You'll find wines from all over the world; not just Italy. It's usually possible to taste some wines and you may be given the odd free gift, but if you do splash out and buy you'll find the red, fruity Montepulciano to be good value for money, and travels well.

Portoricco
Corso Vittorio Emanuele II, 13 (B2)
☎ 06 69 94 22 44.

This old-fashioned shop is where you'll find the best in Italian confectionery, such as the classic chocolate *Baci* ('kisses'), which those in love give to each other – remembering to read the quotations about love inside the wrapper; the *cremini* by Fiat, made from a chocolate so good it can only be matched by the Gianduia from Caffarel, and the romantically-named *Elisir D'Amore* ('elixir of love') and *Promessi Sposi* ('fiancés').

Bottega del Vino da Bleve
Via Santa Maria del Pianto, 9A (C3)
☎ 06 686 59 70.

Many countries produce wine, but

whilst you're in Italy, you must of course try the Italian wines. There's a good range of prices. There are two kinds of Italian wine: DOC (*denominazione di origine controllata*), which is a guarantee of the type of vine and the provenance of the wine, and DOCG (*denominazione di origine controllata e garantita*), which is a much sought-after accreditation and accorded to only a few wines, such as the Chianti Classico and the Brunello di Montalcino.

A TASTE OF ROME

You can find as many as 300 types of bread on sale in Rome, each made for a specific use or occasion. To name but a few, there's *pane casareccio* ideal for *bruschetta, rosetta*, a small rose-shaped roll, *ciriola*, and *sfilatino*, ideal for making up panini (sandwiches). Chocolate lovers should remember to take back home

some *Baci* ('kisses') made by Perugina. These are small chocolates created in 1922, which under their silver wrapping contain a famous quotation about love. Great for breaking the ice with the loved one of your choice.

Volpetti
Via della Scrofa, 31 (C2)
☎ 06 574 23 52.

This is where Italians can come in autumn to buy white truffles, which cost more than their weight in gold, or the less rare and expensive black ones. There's an abundant choice of charcuterie, including the *Norcino* at L19,000 per kg (2.2lb), and the *salame aquilano* at L32,000 per kg (2.2lb). Both of these go well with a slice of slightly salted Tuscan bread. Ham would also make a good souvenir and will cost less than at home. That said, don't expect the *parmigiano* (parmesan cheese) or the *Prosciuto di Parma* to be cheap.

Nightlife

It may well be true that we have to 'see Naples and die', but you also owe it to yourselves to experience and enjoy Rome. So what's best to do at night in Rome? Partly, of course, it depends on the time of year. Summer evenings are particularly pleasant, when classical or jazz concerts, operas, films, ballets, and theatre are held outdoors, in piazzas and gardens, or even against a spectacular backdrop of Roman antiquity. You can also let off steam in one of Rome's many nightclubs, or if you prefer a rest from any form of excursion, simply take a seat on a café *terrasse*, have a drink or an ice-cream, and watch the world go by.

LIVING ROMAN-STYLE

Romans usually have dinner after 9.30pm, and shows start at about the same time. During the summer, it's a good idea to dress lightly, as temperatures can be very high (25-35ºC/75-95ºF) and don't go down much during the night. It's also advisable not to go out with showy jewellery, and passports and plane tickets should be left in the hotel. The liveliest areas in the evenings are Trastevere, around Piazza Navona, and Campo dei Fiori – a good place for dinner, ice-cream or a drink. The trendiest nightclubs are to be found a little outside the centre in areas like Testaccio (Metro Piramide) and Piazza Vittorio (Metro Vittoriano).

WHAT'S ON

All night-owls buy *Roma C'e, Il manuale della settimana in città* (L2,000). It's comprehensive and includes an English-language section. On Thursdays, the daily national newspaper, *La Repubblica*, brings out a supplement, *Trova Roma*. Further practical, though brief, English-language information is to be found in the two bi-monthly magazines, *Wanted in Rome and Metropolitan*, which are on sale in the news kiosks of Piazza Navona and Via Veneto. The weekly listings magazine, *Città Aperta*, is useful and also has an English language section. And in case you don't know what to do with your offspring, here are details of babysitting agencies:

Bacchetta magica
☎ 06 44 24 10 50.

Work Agency
☎ 06 583 67 07.

Evelyn
☎ 06 574 74 44.

TICKETS

If you want tickets to a play, concert or sporting event, a number of agencies can assist you (closed Sat. pm and Sun., payment by credit card):

Pronto Spettacolo:
☎ 06 39 38 72 97.

Anteprima:
☎ 06 474 38 24.

Futura Service:
☎ 06 72 22 51 33.

Romacomoda:
☎ 06 854 84 55.

Babilonia: Via del Corso, 185 ☎ 06 678 66 41.

Prenoticket
(rock, pop and jazz) :
☎ 06 52 20 03 42.

Roman Cultural Association:
☎ 06 372 39 56.

Booking isn't a common practice in Italy, partly because theatres don't accept telephone bookings and concert seats are sold on the spot. Agencies will charge about 10% commission on ticket prices.

For legal reasons, a number of nightclubs require you to have a membership card (*tessera*), which you can purchase at the door. The card admits you and entitles you to a free drink, though the second could set you back L20,000.

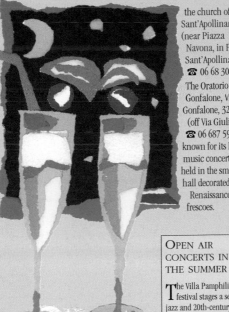

CHURCH CONCERTS

In accordance with a decree by Pope John Paul II, church concerts are reserved without exception for sacred music, and can only be held after the last evening mass. Their schedules are displayed in the city centre.

The most well-known include the concert in St Peter's on 5 December by the orchestra of RAI (the national TV and radio company), and the Sistine chapel choir singing mass celebrated by the Pope on St Peter's day.

On New Year's Eve, the *Te Deum* is sung in the Gesu church, and on Sundays you can hear Gregorian chants in the church of Sant'Apollinare (near Piazza Navona, in Piazza Sant'Apollinare, 49, ☎ 06 68 30 37).

The Oratorio del Gonfalone, Via del Gonfalone, 32 (off Via Giulia), ☎ 06 687 59 52, is known for its Baroque music concerts held in the small hall decorated with Renaissance frescoes.

OPEN AIR CONCERTS IN THE SUMMER

The Villa Pamphili music festival stages a series of jazz and 20th-century music concerts in the gardens of the villa (Via di San Pancrazio, open from dawn to dusk, buses 41, 75, or 144).

L'Accademia di Santa Cecilia organises concerts in the beautiful setting of the nymphaeum of Villa Giulia (Piazzale di Via Giulia, 9, ☎ 06 322 65 71, buses 52 or 926 towards Viale Buozzi, 95, 490).

L'Associazione Musicale Romana organises the 'Serenate in chiostro', in the cloister of Santa Maria della Pace (Vicolo dell'Arco della Pace, 5, ☎ 06 68 61 56) right in the heart of the historic city centre (around L20,000).

Until 1995, the Rome opera company would put on lavish shows featuring, for example, real elephants for Verdi's *Aïda*, when staged in the ancient setting of the Baths of Caracalla. Nowadays, shows that endanger ancient monuments are strictly forbidden.

CAFÉS

Rome without its cafés, ice-cream parlours, *pasticcerie* or wine bars would be totally unimaginable. Whether for a swift *espresso* or *cappuccino* taken standing at the counter, or a pre-dinner aperitif savoured amidst 19th-century elegance or on a cool *terrasse*, or even one last glass sipped in one of the many *enoteche* (wine bars) open 7.30pm-2.30am, there's always a perfect place to go if you're thirsty or want a break.

Caffè Greco
Via Condotti, 86 (C1)
Mon.-Sat. 8am-8.45pm,
closed on bank holidays and
1-21 Aug.

'A narrow, smoke-filled room with low ceilings, without a hint of refinement, but comfortable. Serving food and refreshment that is almost always good and cheap,' as Taine, the 19th-century French writer, described it in his 'Voyage to Italy'. Since 1864, many things have changed. The Greco has now grown more attractive, with a great frescoed landscape of Roman ruins on the wall, small chandeliers hanging from the ceiling, and waiters dressed in tails.

Café della Pace
See p.37, Piazza Navona:
the show goes on (B2)

Rosati
Piazza del Popolo (C1)
8am-11pm.

With its ideally-located *terrasse* facing the rise of the Pincio, this was for years the meeting place for Romans, long before the Tre Scalini on Piazza Navona. Even 20 years ago, regulars included painters and writers, now replaced by budding stars and TV presenters. A lively place, especially towards the end of the

PASTICCERIA

GELATI

ENGLISH E AMERICAN DRINKS

LIQUORI

afternoon. But the prices are extortionate.

Capranica
Piazza Capranica (C2).

This is an old-style café (and snack bar-restaurant) a stone's throw from the Pantheon that does a speciality called the *capranica*. That's the house

name for a small strong *espresso* with an added dose of melted chocolate that blends excellently with the coffee. Not to be missed.

Pasticceria bella napoli
Corso Vittorio Emanuele, 246 (B2).

Naples probably makes the best patisserie in Italy and you can try some here in a peaceful setting. There's the *Sfogliatelle ricce* and *Sfogliatelle frolle*, or the *Tarallucci*, *Struffoli* (usually eaten at Christmas), *Zeppole* (for the *Carnevale* celebrations around *Epiphany*) and *Pastiera* (for Easter).

Trastevere
Baretti
Via Garibaldi, 27 (B3)
8am-11pm, closed Sun.

With views of the sky above the Janiculum Hill and over the rooftops of Trastevere, the terraces of this café are a lovely place to come for breakfast or an

aperitif. In the room at the back they have a 1960s juke-box that quietly plays hits from the period.

Bibli
Via dei Fienaroli, 28 (B3).

This bookshop-café is a great place for brunch on a Sunday morning. Sitting cosily surrounded by books as you flick through the Roman press, you can enjoy a late Italian breakfast. You could of course forget the papers and log on to the Internet as you sip your *cappuccino*.

Piazza di Spagna
Caffè Vittoria
Via Vittoria, 3 (C1)
10am-10pm.

This is the perfect winter café: wood panelling, marble-topped tables, a bunch of flowers adorning the counter, and a smart clientele taking a break from the local boutiques, all in an intimate atmosphere, which may not be typically Roman, but does make it inviting. More of a tearoom, to visit after some shopping.

ICE-CREAM PARLOURS

Giolitti
Via Uffici del Vicario, 40 (C2)
7am-10pm.

This long-established café (founded in 1900) is rightly famous for its ice-cream, which continues to be by far the best in the city centre. They are also particularly proud of their sorbets. The neo-Louis XVI-style tearoom retains its old-fashioned charm, but there is no obligation to consume on the premises.

San Crespino
Via della Panetteria, 42 (D2)
Closed Tue.

Tucked behind the Trevi Fountain, this minuscule ice-cream parlour is popular with Romans for the delicacy of the flavours on offer, many of which are quite unusual. Here's your opportunity to try ginger, cinnamon, nougat and caramel, giandula lemon, and others. Truly a delicious experience.

San Giovanni
Barchiesi e Figli, Via La Spezia, 100 1A (not on map).

According to the *Gambero Rosso* guide (the authoritative gastronomic guide to Rome), this family-run establishment makes the most 'important', i.e. the best, ice-cream. Though you'll be spoilt for choice, you could always try the *visciole* (sour cherry) sorbet or the chestnut ice-cream, to name but two of the flavours which San Giovanni deem their house specialities.

Largo Argentina
Alberto Pica Via della Seggiola, 12 (B3)
10am-10pm, closed Sun.

Certificates of 'Prizes for Excellence' adorn the walls of this ice-cream parlour, where you'll find 50 different choices of flavour. Traditional flavours are sold alongside rarer versions, such as Amalfi lemon, cinnamon, rice, shrimp, and even gorgonzola. They may seem like a strange choice at first, but don't worry – they're delicious.

WINE BARS
(ENOTECHE)

Wine bars have become popular in the last 10 years. Now there are more and more of them and some offer a very wide choice of wines, and not only Italian wines. You can buy a bottle and nibble on some canapés, or have lunch or dinner there (they often stay open until late).

Cul de Sac

**Piazza Pasquino, 73 (B2)
6.30pm-12.30am Mon.,
12.30-3pm and 6.30pm-
12.30am Tue.-Sun.**

This wine bar close by Piazza Navona is still the best in Rome and has one of the best cellars as it has some 1,400 wines. Amongst other things, you can try their *bocconcini di manzo*

(beef snacks with sauce). Note that the tables can only seat up to four.

Trastevere

Ferrara

**Via del Moro, 1 (B3)
8.30pm-1am. Mar.-Sept.,
closed Sun.**

A good place for night-owls as this big wine bar stays open late. The wine list mentions over 200 wines, which can be tried with a salad or with some cheese. When it is warm you can eat and drink outside.

Bevitoria

**Piazza Navona, 72 (B2)
11am-1am Mon.-Sat.**

Add a cultural side to this visit – the cellars are housed in the ruins of Domitian's theatre. To accompany the wine-tasting,

you can order *crostini* (small pieces of toasted bread with duck paté) or charcuterie.

ITALIAN WINE
*'A meal without wine is like
a day without sunshine.'* Anon

Wine in Italy, like bread, is no less important for being taken for granted, but it's a local, even a family affair. The sheer quantity produced each year can even surpass that of France and in the region of Puglia more wine is made in a year than in the whole of Australia. In some restaurants, the *vino di casa* is sold without a label, this being their own production and not subject to duty under Italian law.

An Evening Stroll

If your feet aren't too tired and you're not tempted by a show or a nightclub, here's a suggestion for a walk that should last about an hour. And as you'll see during your stay, wandering through the streets is also popular with the Romans.

Start from the **church of Santa Maria della Pace** to be found on the piazza of the same name laid out by Piero da Cortona in 1656. He was also the architect who built a new façade for the church, which was a first of its kind as it protruded onto the square with a circular portico. The beauty of the church also attracts drunks and tramps, who often congregate on its steps.

Follow the side of the church up Via Arco della Pace and walk through Piazza di Montevecchio, a very theatrical piazza, where an excellent restaurant sets out its tables in summer. Take Via della Pace, then Via di Parione, which lends its name to the neighbourhood – one of the oldest and most picturesque in Rome. Notice the attractive 16th-century palazzo on the right, the birthplace of

Pope Sixtus V. Cross Via del Governo Vecchio and Corso Vittorio by taking Via Sora until you reach Via dei Cappellari, a very long, dark alley which has retained its medieval charm. During the daytime, it bustles with the activity of craftsmen and small traders, but all trace of these disappear in the evening and it becomes easy to picture how life must have been.

Via dei Cappellari leads onto Campo dei Fiori, which is very lively at night. You can pause to catch your breath at the **Drunken Ship** (no. 20) and

La piazza della Rotonda, by night.

try a small *amaro* (a digestif made from plants) or a beer, as it's a Roman pub, or have dinner at the **Campo dei Fiori restaurant**. There's also a small bookshop that stays open until 11pm and is popular with young people. Now take the street to the left of the Farnese cinema,

Via del Biscione, and admire **Palazzo Pio Righetti**, its window frames heavily decorated with menacing birds of prey, the family emblem. Continue going in the same direction towards Largo Pallaro, then take Via dei Chiavari, cross the Corso Vittorio for the second time and don't

forget to have a look at **Palazzo Massimo** (built by Peruzzi in 1532) with its unique curved façade that follows the contours of Domitian's Odeon (used for concerts).

On the left of Corso Vittorio you'll see the splendid **Palazzo della Cancelleria** (Chancery Palace) attributed to Bramante (1444-1514), which houses the papal chancery. This means the building is part of the Vatican territory, and thus only subject to papal authority, in accordance with the Lateran Treaty (1929).

Opposite is the **Palazzo Braschi**, at the southern end of **Piazza Navona**, which, since 1949, houses the Museum of Rome. Walk around this rather ungainly building and you'll find yourself in Piazza Navona. Now all that remains for you to do is to find a seat at one of the cafés.

More handy words and phrases

USEFUL EXPRESSIONS
I am sorry
Mi dispiace
I don't know
Non lo so
How?
Come?
Pardon me?
Prego?
Could you repeat that?
Può ripetere quello per favore?
My name is…
Mi chiamo…
A lot
Molto
Enough
Abbastanza
Nothing
Niente

AT THE HOTEL
Hotel
Albergho
Bed & breakfast/ guesthouse
Pensione
I have a reservation
Ho una prenotazione
…for three people
…per tre persone
…for three nights
…per tre notti
with a double bed
con un letto matrimoniale
with twin beds
con due letti
Is breakfast included?
E compresa la prima colazione?
We are leaving tomorrow morning
Partiamo domani mattina
Suitcase
Valigia

IN THE RESTAURANT
I would like…
Vorrei…

What is the dish of the day?
Qual'è il piatto del giorno?
I would just like something to drink
Vorrei solo bere qualcosa
Wine list
Lista dei vini
Non smoking
Non Fumatori
Baked
Al forno
Grilled
Alla griglia
Poached
Cotto in bianco
Fried
Fritto
Steamed
Al vapore

MEAT AND FISH
Meat
Carne
Bacon
Pancetta
Sausage
Salsiccia
Shellfish/seafood
Molluschi/Frutta di mare
Cod
Merluzzo
Salmon
Salmone

VEGETABLES
Courgettes
Zucchini
Aubergines/eggplants
Melanzane
French beans
Fagiolini
Spinach
Spinaci
Mushrooms
Funghi
Tomato
Pomodoro

Potatoes
Patate

SUNDRIES
Crisps/peanuts
Patatine/noccioline americane
Salt/pepper
Sale/pepe
Mustard
Senape
Sugar
Zucchero
Rice
Riso
Egg
Uovo
Toast
Pane tostato

DRINKS
A glass of…
Un bicchiere di…
Tea with milk/lemon
Thè con latte/limone
Fruit juice
Succo di frutta
Hot chocolate
Cioccolata
Sparkling water
Acqua frizzante

NUMBERS
1 Uno
2 Due
3 Tre
4 Quattro
5 Cinque
6 Sei
7 Sette
8 Otto
9 Nove
10 Dieci
11 Undici
12 Dodici
13 Tredici
14 Quattordici
15 Quindici
16 Seidici

17 Diciasette
18 Diciotto
19 Diciannove
20 Venti

TIME AND DATES
Morning/afternoon/evening
La mattina/il pomeriggio/la sera
Yesterday/today/tomorrow
Ieri/oggi/domani

DAYS OF THE WEEK
Monday
Lunedì
Tuesday
Martedì
Wednesday
Mercoledì
Thursday
Giovedì
Friday
Venerdì
Saturday
Sabato
Sunday
Domenica

IN THE TOWN
Can you tell me the way to…?
Per andare a…?
What time does it open?
A che ora apre?
What time does it close?
A che ora chiude?
Here/there
Qui/là
Near/far
Vicino/lontano
Opposite
Di fronte
Next to
Accanto a
On the left/on the right
A sinistra/a destra
Straight on
Sempre dritto
Entrance/Exit
Entrata/Uscita
Change money
Cambiare
Bureau de change
Cambio
Traveller's cheque
Assegno turistico
Cash machine
Bancomat
Post box
Cassetta
Stamp
Francobollo
Telephone
Telefono

TRAVELLING
I want to go to…
Voglio andare a…
Do I need to change?
Devo cambiare?
Which platform does it leave from?
Da quale binario parte?
Bus/coach station
Stazione di autobus
Bus stop
Fermata d'autobus
Airport
Aeroporto
Taxi rank
Posteggio di taxi
Car
Macchina
Bicycle
Bicicletta
On foot
A piedi
Passport
Passaporto
Timetable
Orario
Left luggage
Deposito bagagli

SHOPPING
It's too expensive
E troppo caro
Where can I find…?
Dove posso trovare…?

SHOPPING FOR CLOTHES AND ACCESSORIES
Bag
Borsa
Belt
Cintura
Blouse
Camicetta
Bracelet
Braccialetto
Coat
Cappotto
Dress
Vestito
Earring
Orecchino
Hat
Capello
Leather
Cuoio
Jacket
Giacca
Jeweller
Gioielliere, orefice
Lingerie
Biancheria intima
Purse
Portamonete
Ring
Anello
Scarf
Sciarpa
Silk
Seta
Socks (or stockings)
Calze
Shirt
Camicia
Shoes
Scarpe
Skirt
Gonna
Suit
Vestito
Sweater
Maglione, golf
T-shirt
Maglietta
Trousers
Pantaloni
Tie
Cravatta
Tights
Collant
Wallet
Portafoglio

Conversion tables for clothes shopping

Note that in Italy 'size' has two different translations. For clothes 'la taglia' is size; for shoes, size is 'il numero'.

Women's sizes

Shirts/dresses

U.K	U.S.A	EUROPE
8	6	36
10	8	38
12	10	40
14	12	42
16	14	44
18	16	46

Sweaters

U.K	U.S.A	EUROPE
8	6	44
10	8	46
12	10	48
14	12	50
16	14	52

Shoes

U.K	U.S.A	EUROPE
3	5	36
4	6	37
5	7	38
6	8	39
7	9	40
8	10	41

Men's sizes

Shirts

U.K	U.S.A	EUROPE
14	14	36
$14^{1/2}$	$14^{1/2}$	37
15	15	38
$15^{1/2}$	$15^{1/2}$	39
16	16	41
$16^{1/2}$	$16^{1/2}$	42
17	17	43
$17^{1/2}$	$17^{1/2}$	44
18	18	46

Suits

U.K	U.S.A	EUROPE
36	36	46
38	38	48
40	40	50
42	42	52
44	44	54
46	46	56

Shoes

U.K	U.S.A	EUROPE
6	8	39
7	9	40
8	10	41
9	10.5	42
10	11	43
11	12	44
12	13	45

More useful conversions

1 centimetre	0.39 inches	1 inch	2.54 centimetres
1 metre	1.09 yards	1 yard	0.91 metres
1 kilometre	0.62 miles	1 mile	1. 61 kilometres
1 litre	1.76 pints	1 pint	0.57 litres
1 gram	0.35 ounces	1 ounce	28.35 grams
1 kilogram	2.2 pounds	1 pound	0.45 kilograms

This guide was written by **Domitilla Cavalletti** in collaboration with Betty der Andreassian and Anne Lehœrff
Translated by **Sam Richard** Design English edition **Vanessa Byrne**
Project manager and copy editor **Margaret Rocques**
Series editor **Liz Coghill**
Additional research and assistance: Jane Moseley, Jenny Piening, Dave McCourt, Natalie Lowe and Christine Bell

We have done our best to ensure the accuracy of the information contained in this guide. However, addresses, phone numbers, opening times etc. inevitably do change from time to time, so if you find a discrepancy please do let us know. You can contact us at: hachetteuk@orionbooks.co.uk or write to us at Hachette UK, address below.

Hachette UK guides provide independent advice. The authors and compilers do not accept any remuneration for the inclusion of any addresses in these guides.

Please note that we cannot accept any responsibility for any loss, injury or inconvenience sustained by anyone as a result of any information or advice contained in this guide.

Photo acknowledgements

Inside pages: **Stéphane Frances** : pp. 2 (c.l., b.r.), 3, 12 (b.r.), 13 (t.l., t.r.), 14 (b.), 15 (t.d), 16, 17, 19 (t., b.), 20 (b.r.), 23 (c.l., c.r.), 24 (b.l.), 25 (c.l., b.r.), 28 (c.l.), 29, 34 (b.), 35 (t.l., c.l., b.r.), 36 (c.r.), 37 (t.l.), 38 (b.l.), 39, 40 (c.l.), 41 (t., c., b.l., b.r.), 42 (b.l.), 43 (t.c., c.c., b.), 44 (t.l., c.d), 46 (b.l.), 47 (c.l.), 48, 49 (c.l., c.r., b.), 50, 51 (t., c., b.), 52, 53 (t.c., b.l., b.r.), 54, 55, 56 (b.l.), 57 (b.) 58 (c.l., b.), 59 (c.l., b.), 60 (b.r.), 61 (t.), 62, 63, 64, 65 (t.r., t.c., c.l., b.l.), 68, 69, 72 (c.r.), 73 (c.l., c.r., b.c.), 74 (c.l., b.), 75, 76 (t.r., c.), 77 (t.l., c.r.), 83 (b.), 85 (t.), 86 (b.r.), 91 (t.r.), 92 (b.r.), 93 (t.r., c.c.), 94 (t.), 99 (t.r.), 103 (c.l.), 111 (c.), 114 (t. bottle), 115 (c., b.l.), 118, 119 (t.l., c.), 120 (c.), 121 (t., c.r.), 122; **Laurent Grandadam** : pp. 2 (t.r.), 12 (b.l.), 13 (c.l., b.r.), 14 (t., b.r.), 18 (c.l.), 19 (c.r.), 20 (t., b.l.), 21 (c.), 22 (b.l.), 23 (b.), 26 (c., b.r.), 27 (c.r., b.), 35 (c.), 37 (t.c.), 38 (c.r.), 41 (t.r.), 42 (c.r.), 43 (c.l., t.r.), 45 (b.), 46 (t.r.), 47 (c.c.), 49 (t.), 57 (b.r.), 58 (c.r.), 61 (c.l., c.r., b.), 65 (c.r.), 71 (b.), 72 (t., c.l., b.r.), 73 (b.r.), 74 (t.l.), 76 (t.l., t.c., c.r., b.), 77 (b.), 82 (b.r.), 83 (t.), 84, 85 (b.), 86 (c.r.), 87 (t.l., b.r.), 88 (b.), 89 (t.c., t.r., b.), 90 (b.), 89 (t.c., c.l.), 90 (b.l., b.c), 91 (c.r., b.l., b.r.), 93 (t.), 94, 95, 96 (b.r.), 97 (t., b.l.), 99 (c.l., c.c.), 100 (t.), 102 (b.l.), 103 (t.l.), 105 (c.r.), 108 (t., b.r.), 109 (t.r.), 110 (c.), 111 (t.l., c.l., c.r., b.), 112 (b.l.), 113 (c., c.l.), 114 (t. meat, c.l., b.), 115 (t.l. and r., c.r.), 119 (t.r., b.), 120 (t.), 121 (b.), 123 (t.); **Éric Guillot** : pp. 47 (t.l.), 53 (c.l.), 73 (c.r.), 84 (t.l.), 89 (c.l.), 90 (c.l.), 94 (c.r.), 98 (b.r.), 101 (b.c.), 103 (c.r. , b.c.), 104 (c.r.), 105 (b.r.), 106 (b.r.), 107, 108 (b.l.), 109 (t.l.), 112 (b.c.); **D. Cleek** : pp. 14 (t.), 27 (b.), 35 (c.), 42 (c.r.), 43 (c.l.), 57 (b.r.), 117 (b.); **Pawel Wysocki** : pp. 36 (b.), 44 (b.l.), 56 (c.r.), 57 (t.l., t.c.), 60 (b.l.); **Robert Leslie** : pp. 25 (c.r.), 27 (t.l.); **Laurent Parrault** : pp. 18 (b.), 21 (t.r.), 47 (b.), 91 (b.c.), 100 (b.), 104 (t.), 110 (t.), 112 (t., c.); **Christian Sarramon** : pp. 15 (c.), 26 (t.), 27 (c.r.), 28 (b.), 37 (t.r.); **Hachette Livre** : pp. 10, 11 (t.l.), 15 (b.), 34 (c.), 37 (b.c. *Droits réservés*), 51 (t.r.), 104 (b.r.), 105 (b.l.); *Droits réservés* : p. 11 (t.r.); **B. Magli** : p. 22 (b.r.); **Fendissime** : p. 82 (c., b.c.); **Prada** : p. 82 (t.l.); **F. & B. Caggi** : p. 83 (c.l.); **Arsenale** : p. 85 (c.); **P. Claggi** : p. 87 (t.c.); **R. Zabban** : p. 86 (b.c.); **Davide Cenci** : p. 88 (t.r.); **Bruno Piatelli** : p. 89 (c.l.), **Brugnoli** : p. 95 (t.r.), **B. Magli** : p. 95 (c.r., b.l.); **La Perla** : p. 98 (t., b.l.); **Sermoneta** : p. 101 (t.); **Catello d'Auria Cuanti Cauze** : p. 101 (b.); **Fontana Arte** : p. 103 (t.r.); **Acanto** : p. 105 (t.); **B.B.K.** : p. 109 (c.l.). **S. Ferragamo** : p. 94 (b.l.).

Front cover: **Pawel Wysocki** t.l., t.r., c.l., c.c., c.r.; **Image Bank - Bokelberg** t.c., b.c.; **Pix M. Goldman** c. (figures); **Stéphane Frances** b.l., b.r.

Back cover: **Christian Sarramon** c.l.; **Éric Guillot** t.c. (bag); **Stéphane Frances** t.r., b.

Illustrations: Pascal Garnier (with the exception of p. 106 (t.), Monique Prudent)

Cartography © Hachette Tourisme

First published in the United Kingdom in 2000 by Hachette UK

© English Translation, revised and updated, Hachette UK 2000
© Hachette Livre (Hachette Tourisme) 1998

Distributed in the United States of America by Sterling Publishing Co., Inc. 387 Park Avenue South, New York, NY 10016-8810

A CIP catalogue for this book is available from the British Library

ISBN 1 84202 003 X

Hachette UK, Cassell & Co., The Orion Publishing Group, Wellington House, 125 Strand, London WC2R 0BB

Printed and bound in Italy by Vincenzo Bona

If you're staying longer than a long weekend and want to discover places other than those previously mentioned, the following pages should provide you with a wide choice of hotels, bars and restaurants, classified by price. Though you may be able to turn up at the door of a restaurant and moments later order your meal, remember to book your hotel several days in advance (see page 66). Enjoy your stay!

STAYING ON
A LITTLE LONGER

Prices given are for double rooms with en-suite bathroom or shower (except for the cheaper establishments) and breakfast. These are high-season prices. If you go during the off-peak season, prices could be significantly lower.

OVER L450,000

Bernini Bristol
Piazza Barberini, 23
☎ 06 488 30 51
📠 06 482 42 66
Double room: L528,000.
A benchmark in Roman hotels for over a century.

De La Ville
Via Sistina, 69
☎ 06 673 31
📠 06 678 42 13
Double room: L583,000-L641,000.
Ask for a room on the 6th floor (all have a terrace with panoramic views).

Eden
Via Ludovisi, 49
☎ 06 47 81 21
📠 06 482 15 84
Double room: L600,000-L700,000.
A very comfortable hotel with a terrace garden overlooking the whole of Rome.

Del Sole al Pantheon
Piazza della Rotonda, 63
☎ 06 678 04 41
📠 06 69 94 06 89
Double room: L470,000.
A delightful location in front of the Pantheon. Has bathrooms with hydromassage shower.

Hilton
Via Cadiolo, 101
☎ 06 350 91
📠 06 35 09 22 41
Double room: L475,000-L620,000
Suites: L1-3,000,000.
A luxurious hotel with exemplary service.

Holiday Inn Crowne
Piazza della Minerva, 69
☎ 06 69 94 18 88
📠 06 679 41 65
Double room: L590,000.
The guaranteed luxury of a household name located in the heart of Rome.

Holiday Inn St. Peter's
Via Aurelia Antica, 417
☎ 06 66 42
📠 06 663 71 90
Double room: L480,000.
An attractive hotel to the north of St Peter's. Has tennis court and swimming pool available to guests.

Lord Byron
Via Giuseppe de Notaris, 5
☎ 06 322 45 41
📠 06 322 04 05
Double room: L520-550,000.
Away from the bustle of the city centre – for those who love peace and quiet.

L300,000-L450,000

Barocco
Piazza Barberini, 9
☎ 06 487 20 01
📠 06 48 59 94
Double room: L380,000.
Great attention has been paid to the decoration and furnishing of this hotel. Breakfast is served on the terrace.

Britannia
Via Napoli, 64
☎ 06 488 31 53
📠 06 488 23 43
Double room: L300,000.
A high class hotel near the central station, Stazione Centrale Roma Termini.

Hotel d'Inghilterra
Via Bocca del Leone, 14
☎ 06 699 81
📠 06 69 92 22 43
Double room: L380,000-L450,000.
This was the favourite hotel of the artists and writers on the 'Grand Tour' in the 19th century. Probably Rome's most renowned hotel.

Farnese
Via Alessandro Farnese, 30
☎ 06 321 25 53
📠 06 321 51 29
Double room: L340,000.
Has the atmosphere of a luxury villa very close to the centre of Rome.

Massimo d'Azeglio
Via Cavour, 18
☎ 06 488 06 46
📠 06 482 73 86
Double room: L385,000.
Not far from the Colosseum, for those who love turn of the century decor.

Pensione Scalinata di Spagna
Piazza Trinita dei Monti, 17
☎ 06 69 94 08 96
📠 06 69 04 05 98
Double room: L380,000.
A family atmosphere reigns in this pensione near one of the most famous stairways in the world and the Villa Borghese.

Raphael
Largo Febo, 2
☎ 06 68 28 31
📠 06 687 89 93
Double room: L370,000-540,000.
Like Claudia Cardinale, choose this hotel 100m from Piazza Navona and you can't go wrong.

Santa Chiara
Via di Santa Chiara, 21
☎ 06 687 29 79
📠 06 687 31 44
Double room: L300,000.
A very comfortable hotel ideally located behind the Pantheon.

Viminale
Via Cesare Balbo, 31
☎ 06 488 19 80
📠 06 487 20 18
Double room: L308,000.
An attentive welcome is guaranteed here. Ask for a room with a balcony and view onto Santa Pudenziana.

L250,000-L300,000

Arcangelo
Via Boezio, 15
☎ 06 687 41 43

☎ 06 689 30 50
Double room: L250,000.
The owner's distinctive personal touch is evident in this hotel not far from Castel Sant'Angelo.

Carriage
Via delle Carrozze, 36
☎ 06 699 01 24
🖷 06 678 82 79
Double room: L295,000.
Admirably located near the Spanish Steps.

Celio
Via dei Santi Quattro, 25/c
☎ 06 70 49 53 33
🖷 06 709 63 77
Double room: L290,000.
An elegant hotel with due attention paid to the slightest detail.

Galles
Via Castro Pretorio, 66
☎ 06 445 47 41
🖷 06 445 69 93
Double room: L250,000.
A charming hotel near the university.

Gregoriana
Via Gregoriana, 18
☎ 06 679 42 69
🖷 06 67 87 42 58
Double room: L280,000.
A renovated former convent now offering good value for money near the Spanish Steps.

Internazionale
Via Sistina, 79
☎ 06 69 94 18 23
🖷 06 678 47 64
Double room: L295,000.
Some rooms with a view available in this former convent not far from the Trinità dei Monti.

Locarno
Via della Penna, 22
☎ 06 361 08 41
🖷 06 321 52 49
Double room: L280,000.
Splendid Liberty-style hotel right behind Piazza del Popolo. The terrace has panoramic views.

Marghera
Via Marghera, 29
☎ 06 445 42 37
🖷 06 446 25 39
Double room: L290,000.
A clean, well-maintained hotel convenient for the station.

Oxford
Via Buoncompagni, 89
☎ 06 42 82 89 52
🖷 06 481 53 49
Double room: L270,000.
Has basic, but more spacious than average, rooms.

Regno
Via del Corso, 330
☎ 06 679 21 19
🖷 06 678 92 39
Double room: L270,000.
An unexpected haven of peace on one of Rome's busiest shopping streets.

Richmond
Largo Corrado Ricci, 36
☎ 06 69 94 12 56
🖷 06 69 94 14 54
Double room: L290,000.
Little touches (welcome gift, individual style to each room) may help you to overlook the perhaps excessive rates in this hotel opposite the Imperial Forum.

Sant'Anna
Borgo Pio, 133
☎ 06 68 80 16 02
🖷 06 68 30 87 17
Double room: L250,000.
Located 100m from the Vatican in the village-like Borgo quarter.

Teatro di Pompeo
Largo del Pallaro, 8
☎ 06 687 28 12
🖷 06 880 55 31
Double room L260,000.
It's usually best to reserve in advance for this hotel right by Campo dei Fiori, and popular with academics.

Turner
Via Nomentana, 29
☎ 06 44 25 00 77
🖷 06 44 25 01 65
Double room: L290,000.
All rooms have 'French beds', i.e. extra-wide double beds.

L200,000–250,000

Andreotti
Via Castelfidardo, 55
☎ 06 444 13 01
🖷 06 445 37 77
Double rooms: L200,000.
Some rooms have a sauna. Buffet breakfast.

HOTELS

Bolivar
Via della Cordonata, 6
☎ 06 679 16 14
📠 06 679 10 25
Double room: L235,000.
Offers the pleasure of staying behind the Trajan Forum, but at a premium.

Canada
Via Vicenza, 58
☎ 06 445 77 70
📠 06 445 07 49
Double room: L220,000.
This represents good value for money in the area around the central station.

Croce di Malta
Via Borgognona, 28
☎ 06 679 54 82
📠 06 69 94 02 50
Double room:L240,000.
A somewhat expensive hotel, set in the heart of the area around the Spanish Steps.

De Petris
Via del Boccaccio, 25
☎ 06 481 96 26
📠 06 482 07 33
Double rooms: L220,000-330,000.
Each room is decorated in its own individual style.

Giglio dell'Opera
Via Principe Amedeo, 14
☎ 06 488 02 19
📠 06 487 14 25.
For Italian hospitality in a British setting.

Grifo
Via del Boschetto, 144
☎ 06 487 13 95
📠 06 474 23 23
Double room: L210,000.
A fairly unexceptional hotel, except for the terrace with a panoramic view.

Homs
Via della Vite, 71
☎ 06 679 29 76
📠 06 678 04 82
Double room: L240,000.
Located not far from the Spanish Steps, this hotel has one of the most charming terrace views in Rome.

Impero
Via Viminale, 19
☎ 06 482 00 67

📠 06 483 77 62
Double room: L240,000.
An early 20th-century building converted into a high-class hotel.

Olympic
Via Properzio, 2/a
☎ 06 689 66 50
📠 06 68 30 82 55
Double rooms: L200-250,000.
Excellent value for money and near the Vatican.

Picadilly
Via Magna Grecia, 122
☎ 06 77 20 70 17
📠 06 70 47 66 86
Double room L210,000.
An unexceptional hotel, except for the attractive 8th-floor terrace. In the San Giovanni in Laterano area.

Sant'Anselmo
Piazza di Sant'Anselmo, 2
☎ 06 574 35 47
📠 06 578 36 04
Double room: L230,000.
The charm of an old-fashioned Liberty-style hotel, tucked away amidst the greenery of the Aventine Hill.

Santa Costanza
Viale XXI Aprile, 4
☎ 06 860 06 02
📠 06 860 27 86
Double room: L240,000.
Has three rooms specially-adapted for wheelchair access.

Spring House
Via Mocenigo, 7
☎ 06 39 72 09 48
📠 06 39 72 10 47
Double room L220,000.
Right by the Vatican. Has international daily newspapers available at breakfast.

Venezia
Via Varese, 18
☎ 06 445 71 01
📠 06 495 76 87
Double room: L220,000.
A reliable recently-renovated hotel near the central station.

Villa San Pio
Via di Sant'Anselmo, 19
☎ 06 574 35 47
📠 06 578 36 04
Double room: L230,000.

Some of the rooms are located in the garden of this hotel on the Aventine Hill.

L150,000-L200,000

Arenula
Via Santa Maria de' Calderari, 47
☎ 06 687 95 45
📠 06 689 61 88
Double room: L160,000.
Located in the Ghetto, and therefore ideal for exploring the historic centre on foot.

Augustea
Via Nazionale, 251
☎ 06 488 35 89
📠 06 481 48 72
Double room: L170,000.
A reliable medium-class hotel near the central station.

Campo de' Fiori
Via del Biscione, 6
☎ 06 68 80 68 65
📠 06 687 60 03
Double room: L180,000.
Recently-renovated with two small delightful terraces overlooking Campo dei Fiori.

Erdarelli
Via Due Macelli, 28
☎ 06 679 12 65
📠 06 679 07 05
Double room: L160,000.
A family atmosphere in this centrally-located hotel.

Laurentia
Largo degli Osci, 63
☎ 06 445 02 18
📠 06 445 38 21
Double room: L190,000.
Located near the university. Three of the rooms have wheelchair access.

Porta Maggiore
Piazza di Porta Maggiore, 25
☎ 06 702 79 27
📠 06 702 79 36
Double room: L180,000.
Notice the hall decorated with the remains of Roman sarcophagi. 240 rooms.

Trevi
Viale del Babuccio, 20/21
☎ 06 678 95 63
📠 06 69 94 14 07

Double room: L190,000.
Breakfast is served on the terrace when the weather is fine.

Villa del Parco
Via Nomentana, 110
☎ 06 44 23 77 73
🅕 06 44 23 75 72
Double rooms: L190,000–L215,000.
An early 20th-century building outside the old city.

UNDER L150,000

Adriatic
Via Vitelleschi, 25
☎ 06 68 80 80 80
🅕 06 689 35 52
Double rooms L100,000–L150,000.
This is a bargain – located only 550m/500yds from the Vatican.

Il Piccolo
Via Chiavari, 32
☎ 06 689 32 30
Double room: L130,000.
For shallower pockets.

Sole
Via del Biscione, 76
☎ 06 68 80 68 73
🅕 06 689 37 87
Double rooms: L140,000–L160,000.
Located right in the heart of the historic centre, this is one of the best deals on offer.

HOTELS

The prices indicated are for a complete meal, not including drinks.

A standard Italian meal comprises an *antipasto* (a starter, usually vegetables, charcuterie or seafood), a *primo* (rice or pasta), a *secondo* (meat or fish) eaten with a *contorno* (vegetables or salad) and a *dolce* (a dessert). As you can imagine, it's not unusual to 'lighten' the meal by taking one, if not two, fewer dishes than normal!

Most of the restaurants have intentionally been selected in the historic centre and surrounding areas, with only a few exceptions. It's not uncommon for the cheaper restaurants to accept only cash.

OVER L100,000

Camponeschi
Piazza Farnese, 50/50a
☎ 06 687 49 27
Closed lunchtimes (except for large bookings).
All major credit cards accepted.
This gourmet restaurant by Palazzo Farnese has an excellent wine list, and serves fish specialities.

Les Etoiles
Via Vitelleschi, 34
☎ 06 687 32 33
Open every day
All major credit cards accepted.
The terrace of this hotel restaurant appears to be a garden suspended over the colonnade of St Peter's.

Relais La Piscine
Via G. Mangili, 6
☎ 06 322 39 93
Open every day
All major credit cards accepted
Outside the centre.

A young chef from Brittany has successfully managed to combine some of his native cuisine with Mediterranean recipes.

Relais Le Jardin
Via G. de Notaris, 5
☎ 06 322 04 04
Closed Sun.
All major credit cards accepted
Outside the centre.
This is the restaurant of the Lord Byron hotel, and serves good quality traditional dishes.

La Rosetta
Via della Rosetta, 8
☎ 06 686 10 02
Closed Sat. afternoon, Sun. and the whole of Aug.
This is an excellent fish restaurant, albeit a little expensive.

The Restaurant of the Grand Hotel
Via V. E. Orlando, 3
☎ 06 47 09
Open every day
All major credit cards accepted.
This is the Roman equivalent of the Ritz and has been in existence for more than a century. Dessert menu changed every day.

Sans Souci
Via Sicilia, 20
☎ 06 482 18 14
Closed Mon. afternoon and the whole of Aug.
All major credit cards accepted.
High-class, mainly French dishes. Ideal for after the theatre.

L70,000-100,000

Antica Enoteca Capranica
Piazza Capranica, 99
☎ 06 69 94 09 92
Closed Sat. and Sun. afternoon.
Original cuisine and a well-stocked wine list in a 15th-century palazzo.

Boccondivino
Vicolo della Campana, 11
☎ 06 68 30 71 29
Closed Mon. and the whole of Aug.
Seasonal Mediterranean cuisine. Also fresh fish (and champagne scampi).

Dal Bolognese
Piazza del Popolo, 1
☎ 06 361 14 26
Closed Mon., Sat. and Sun., Jul. and Aug. open Mon.
Cuisine from Emilia, and homemade pasta.

Carlo Menta
Via della Lungaretta, 101
☎ 06 580 37 33
Closed Mon. and lunchtimes.
This is a fish restaurant whose previous regulars included Sinatra and Liz Taylor.

Il Corsaro
Via del Boccaccio, 6
☎ 06 481 79 15
Closed Sun. and the whole of Aug.
Fish dishes a speciality.

Il Convivio
Via dell'Orso, 44
☎ 06 68 69 432
Closed Sun.
The creative cuisine of this restaurant has established a good reputation for itself in the past few years.

Fantasie di Trastevere
Via S. Dorotea, 6
☎ 06 588 16 71
Closed at lunchtimes.
Traditional cooking. Aperitifs can be served in the pleasant courtyard.

Papa Giovanni
Via dei Sediari, 4
☎ 06 68 65 308
Closed Sun.
This restaurant very close to Piazza Navona, is almost an institution in Roman cuisine, to whose renewal it has contributed. The ingredients are bought on the Campo dei Fiori market. Good wine list and list of olive oils.

Ranieri
Via Mario de' Fiori, 26.
☎ 06 69 92 24 15
Closed Sun.
*Serving food since 1843!
Specialities include crêpes à la
Ranieri (pancakes with eight
different cheeses).*

L50,000–
L70,000

Alfredo
Piazza Augusto
Imperatore, 30
☎ 06 687 87 34
Closed Sun.
*Has retained its reputation as
the 'fettuccine empire' for over
half a century.*

Antica Pesa
Via Garibaldi, 18
☎ 06 580 93 36
Closed Sun.
*Occupying a 17th-century
convent in the Trastevere
quarter, with a pleasant
garden.*

Arlu
Borgo Pio, 135
☎ 06 686 89 36
Closed Sun.
*Creative cuisine, including
tonnarelli with orange sauce.*

Bacco
Via di Grottapinta, 8
☎ 06 68 80 53 49
Closed Sun. eve. and
Mon.
*Speciality – squid stuffed with
ricotta cheese.*

Il Buco
Via S. Ignazio, 8
☎ 06 679 32 98
Closed Mon. and the
whole of Aug.
*Serves Tuscan cuisine, including
pappardelle in hare sauce.*

Il Ciak
Vicolo delle Cinque, 21
☎ 06 589 47 74
Closed Mon., lunchtimes
and mid-July to Sept.
*Serves Tuscan cuisine, including
pappardelle with boar or duck
sauce.*

Checo er Carrettiere
Via Benedette, 10
☎ 06 581 70 18
Closed Sun. eve. and
Mon.
*This was fashionable in the
1960s and still serves certain
dishes from that heyday.*

Costanza
Piazza del Paradiso,
63/65
☎ 06 686 17 17
Closed Sun. and the
whole of Aug.
*The house antipasto is a
selection of olives, pâtés,
various vegetables prepared
in olive oil and cream cheese.*

Il Drappo
Vicolo del Malpasso, 9
☎ 06 687 73 65
Closed Sun., lunchtimes,
and the whole of Aug.
*Serves Sardinian cuisine
(artichoke soup) and has an
interior garden.*

Girarrosto Toscano
Piero Bruni
Via Germanico, 56
☎ 06 39 72 57 17
Closed Mon.
*Offers meat dish specialities,
served in large portions.*

Hostaria Antica
Roma
Via Appia Antica, 87
☎ 06 51 32 08 88/
06 59 40 534
Closed Mon. and 2 weeks
in Aug.
*Offers traditional Italian cuisine
but in the surprising decor of
ancient Roman ruins.*

L'Eau Vive
Via Monterone, 85
☎ 06 68 80 10 95
Closed Sun. and the
whole of Aug.
*Owned by a religious order
which lends it an unusual
atmosphere and is a reminder
that men of the cloth certainly
appreciate the joys of the
table.*

La Penna d'Oca
Via della Penna, 53
☎ 06 320 28 98
Closed Sun.
*Has seafood specialities,
including fusilli with courgette
(zucchini) flowers and
clams.*

RESTAURANTS

Peccati di Gola
Piazza de' Ponziani, 7
☎ 06 581 14 529
Closed Mon.
A family restaurant located on an attractive piazza in Trastevere and serving Calabrese cuisine.

Pierluigi
Piazza de' Ricci, 144
☎ 06 68 61 13 02
Closed Mon.
Accepts only Visa and AmEx.
Located on an intimate Renaissance piazza, this restaurant serves high-quality traditional cooking, including fish carpaccio.

Piperno
Via Montede' Cenci, 9
☎ 06 68 80 27 72
Closed Mon., Sun. eve. and the whole of Aug.
On a pretty piazza in the heart of the Ghetto, this is one of the best places to try Jewish-Roman cooking.

Romolo nel giardino della Fornarina
Via di Porta Settimiana, 8
☎ 06 581 82 84
Closed Mon. and for 3 weeks in Aug.
This garden courtyard (with 100-year old vines) is said to be where Raphael used to meet the beautiful Fornarina, of whom he left an elegant portrait. The service is friendly.

Il Sanpietrino
Piazza Costaguti, 15
☎ 06 68 80 64 71.
Closed Sun., lunchtimes, and the whole of Aug.
Good and sometimes creative cooking, e.g. rolled veal with provola and pork cheek.

Le Streghe
Vicolo del Curato, 13
☎ 06 686 13 81
Closed Sun. and the whole of Aug.
Serves original dishes, including spaghetti with broccoli and truffles.

Taverna del Duca
Via di Panico, 83
☎ 06 687 36 66
Closed Mon. and 2 weeks in Aug.
Offers specialities from Southern Italy, such as linguini with cartuccio.

Taverna Giulia
Vicolo dell'Oro, 23
☎ 06 686 97 68
Closed Sun.
Cuisine from Liguria, such as pasta with pesto.

La Veranda del Columbus
Via della Conciliazione, 33
☎ 06 686 54 35
Open every day.
Original dishes, such as fish in breadcrumbs with walnuts. Located in a 15th-century building close to the Vatican.

L30,000-L50,000

Abruzzi
Via del Vaccaro, 1
☎ 06 679 38 97
Closed Sat.
All credit cards except AmEx accepted.
Serves home cooking with Abruzzo influences (risotto with herbs).

Albistro
Via dei Banchi Vecchi, 140
☎ 06 686 52 74
Closed Wed., Sat., and Sun. lunchtime.
No credit cards accepted.
Highly original dishes served a stone's throw from Palazzo Farnese.

Angelino ai Fori
Largo Corrado Ricci, 40
☎ 06 679 11 21
Closed Tue. and Christmas.
Traditional cooking in this restaurant located by the Imperial Forum and once a favourite place of Alec Guiness.

Arancio d'Oro
Via Monte d'Oro, 17
☎ 06 686 50 26
Closed Sun. and 15 Jul.-15 Sep.
The speciality is meat dishes.

L'Archetto a Fontana di Trevi
Via dell'Archetto, 26
☎ 06 678 90 64
Closed Mon.
Offers over 100 choices of pasta dish.

Armando al Pantheon
Salita dei Crescenzi, 31
☎ 06 68 80 30 34
Closed Sat. eve., Sun. and the whole of Aug.
All major credit cards accepted
Traditional Roman cooking, including Roman-style tripe.

Il Capitello
Piazza Campo dei Fiori, 4
☎ 06 68 61 15 50
Open every day.
This is ideal for group meals and has an adjacent pizzeria.

Clochard
Via del Teatro della Pace, 30
☎ 06 68 80 20 29
Closed Mon. lunchtime, and the whole of Jul. and Aug.
The decor is Arte povera, and the cooking traditional Roman. A convenient restaurant for a meal after the show at the nearby theatre.

Colline Emiliane
Via degli Avignonesi, 22
☎ 06 481 75 38
Closed Fri.
No credit cards accepted.
Makes the best tortellini in Rome.

Il Desiderio preso per la Coda
Vicolo della Palomba, 23
☎ 06 68 30 75 22
Closed Mon., lunchtimes, and the whole of Aug.
Serves original dishes in an artistic setting. 'Pasolini' pancakes (with milk, smoked provola and honey).

Le Maschere
Via Monte della Farina, 29
Closed Mon., lunchtimes, and Aug.
Calabrese cuisine, such as pasta with aubergines.

Otello alla Concordia
Via della Croce, 81
☎ 06 679 11 78
Closed Sun.
*A good place to eat in this area
of elegant boutiques.*

La Piazzetta
Via Cardinal Merry del
Val, 16/b
☎ 06 580 62 41
Closed Wed. lunchtime.
*This is a typical Trastevere
trattoria.*

Piccolo Arancio
Vicolo Scanderberg, 112
☎ 06 678 61 39
Closed lunchtimes and
2 weeks in Aug.
*Offers traditional Roman
cooking (including artichokes
cooked in Roman/Jewish way)*

Sora Margherita
Piazza delle Cinque
Scole, 30
686 40 02
Closed Sat., Sun.,
evenings and the whole
of Aug.
No credit cards accepted.
Jewish/Roman cooking.

Vecchia Locanda
Vicolo Sinibaldi, 2
☎ 06 68 80 28 31
Closed Sun.
Good for a quick meal.

Walter
Via del Pellegrino, 107
☎ 06 68 69 361/
06 68 72 776
Closed Mon.
*One of the best places to
see how Italians cook fish.
Try the typical southern Italian
antipasti.*

UNDER
L30,000

Da Baffetto
Via del Governo Vecchio,
114
☎ 06 686 16 17
Closed Sun., lunchtimes
and the whole of Aug.
No credit cards accepted.
*This is the mecca of Roman
pizza so be prepared to wait.*

Il Facocchio
Vicolo della Pelliccia, 29

☎ 06 581 80 50
Closed Sun., lunchtimes
and the whole of Aug.
No credit cards accepted.
*This cultural organisation
provides all its own ingredients.*

Da Felice
Via Mastro Giorgio, 29
☎ 06 574 68 00
Closed Sun. and the
whole of Aug.
This is a typical 1960s trattoria.

Da Giovanni
Via della Lungara, 41
☎ 06 686 15 14
Closed Sun.
No credit cards accepted.
A good trattoria in Trastevere.

**Grotte Teatro di
Pompeo**
Via del Biscione, 73
☎ 06 68 80 36 86
Closed Mon.
*A very welcoming restaurant
serving some of the most
traditional Roman dishes.*

Insalata Ricca
Largo de' Chiavari, 85
☎ 06 68 80 36 56
No credit cards accepted.
*Offers a choice of over 20
salads.*

La Montecarlo
Via dei Savelli, 12
☎ 06 686 18 77
Closed 1-15 Aug.
No credit cards accepted.
*The place to go if Baffetto (of
which this is an offshoot) is
too busy.*

Der Pallaro
Largo del Pallaro, 15
☎ 06 68 80 14 88
Closed Mon. and 2 weeks
in Aug.
No credit cards accepted.
Roman home cooking.

Dar Poeta
Vicolo del Bologna, 45
(corner of Piazza della
Scala)
☎ 06 588 05 16
Closed on Mon. and
lunchtimes.
Accepts Visa.
*Pizzeria serving some original
pizzas (e.g. la Bodrilla – with
apples and orange liqueur).*

RESTAURANTS

La Pollarolla di dell'Omo Mario
Piazza Pollarolla, 25
☎ 06 68 80 16 54
Closed Sun.
Inexpensive, excellent pasta dishes. One of the few local restaurants to open on a Monday.

Da Tonino
Via del Governo Vecchio, 18
0360 24 16 93
Closed Sat. eve., Sun. and Aug.
Typical Roman cooking, with gnocchi (a well-known speciality made from potatoes).

Da Vittorio
Via di San Cosimato, 14/a
☎ 06 580 03 53
Closed Mon. and the second fortnight in Sep.
No credit cards accepted.
Best to book in advance for this tiny pizzeria, reputed for its creative Neapolitan pizzas (try the Imperiale – served cold).

La Zucca Magica
Via dei Barbieri, 23
☎ 06 683 32 07
Closed Sun., Mon., Aug. and Christmas.
Vegetarian cooking.

RESTAURANTS

Antico Caffè della Pace
Piazza della Pace
☎ 06 68 61 216.
A chic and fashionable café in the historic centre.

Bar Navona
Piazza Navona, 67
☎ 06 686 14 02.
If you've already been to the Tre Scalini, or if it's Wednesday, which is closing day at the Tre Scalini.

Bar della Palma
Via della Maddalena, 20/23
☎ 06 68 80 67 52.
A determinedly modern (i.e. neon lights and bright colours) ice cream parlour.

Bar Rotonda
Piazza Rotonda, 68
☎ 06 67 98 719.
Ideal if you want to have an aperitif in front of the Pantheon.

Bear's Pub
Via dei Cappellari, 36
☎ 06 686 54 05
Open 8pm-3am, closed Mon.
Entrance free.
Pub with blues, rock and sometimes piano concerts on the lower floor and a quieter room upstairs.

La Briciola
Via della Lungaretta, 81
☎ 06 581 122 60
Open 8.30pm-2am except Tue.
Entrance free.
An inviting atmosphere, and ideal if you feel like a salad or sandwich with a beer late in the evening.

Café Notegen
Via del Babuino, 159
Tel: 32 00 855.
A place to stop at for a cappuccino after a shopping trip.

Caffè Capranica
Piazza Capranica, 104
☎ 06 679 08 60.
The house speciality is coffee with melted chocolate (the Capranica).

Caffè Greco
Via Condotti, 86
☎ 06 67 82 554.
One of Rome's oldest cafés, and once the haunt of famous writers and artists.

Il Cantiniere di S. Dorotea
Via di S. Dorotea, 9
☎ 06 581 90 25.
A friendly place to listen to jazz and have some wine.

Cavour 313
Via Cavour, 313
☎ 06 678 54 96.
One of Rome's best wine bars, opened at the end of the 1970s.

Clochard
Via del Teatro Pace, 29/30
☎ 06 68 80 20 29
Open 8.30pm-3.30am except Mon.
Entrance free.
At weekend, minimum drink per person L15,000.
Café with singers and dancing. Food also served.

Cul de Sac
Piazza Pasquino, 73
☎ 06 68 80 10 94.
More than 2,000 wines to choose from, and cooking of a high standard.

Dam Dam
Via Bendetta, 17 (Trastevere)
☎ 06 58 96 225.
Open every day 8pm-2am, entrance free.
Bar on two floors, with theme nights. Tue. is usually salsa and Latin music.

Ferrara
Via del Moro, 1/a
☎ 06 580 37 69.
One of the two sister owners is an architect and has redecorated it herself.

Fiocco di Neve
Via del Pantheon, 51
☎ 06 678 60 25.
This tiny place is considered one of the best ice cream makers in Rome. Try it and decide for yourselves.

Il Gelato di San Crispino
Via Acaia, 55/56
☎ 06 70 45 04 12.
The most creative ice cream maker in Rome, and perhaps in the whole of the country. Flavours include cinnamon and ginger.

Giolitti al Vicario
Via Uffici del Vicario, 40
☎ 06 699 12 43.
Everyone comes to this famous ice cream parlour to try some of the 50 flavours.

Il Goccetto
Via dei Banchi Vecchi, 14
☎ 06 686 42 68.
A good choice of wines but only seven tables.

Gran Caffè Vescovio
Piazza Vescovio, 6/b
☎ 06 86 21 10 05.
Has excellent croissants.

Internet café
Via Aubry, 1/a
☎ 06 39 74 27 52
Open 7pm-1am (2am at weekend).
For those who are hooked.

Jenko Caffè
Piazza San Cosimato, 39
☎ 06 58 80 838
Open 9pm-2am, except Mon.
Free entrance.
Various rooms and music. Also has dinner menu.

Rosati
Piazza del Popolo, 4
☎ 06 322 58 59.
One of the most common meeting places around Piazza del Popolo.

Santa Barbara Pub
Largo dei Librari, 82/a
☎ 06 686 74 63
Open 9pm-4am
Free entrance.
A good place for night owls with a Renaissance/South American/Irish pub decor!

Sant'Eustachio
Piazza S. Eustachio, 82
☎ 06 686 13 09.
Famous for coffee – make sure you try the Gran Caffè.

Il Simposio di Constantini
Piazza Cavour, 16
☎ 06 321 15 02.
A good opportunity for wine tasting before visiting the cellars of the adjacent wine shop.

Tazza d'Oro
Via degli Orfani, 84
☎ 06 678 97 92.
Try the granita di caffè (coffee, crushed ice and chantilly cream) as you sit on bags full of coffee beans. Very refreshing in summer.

Tre Scalini
Piazza Navona, 28
☎ 06 68 80 19 96.
The house speciality is the tartufo nero (ice cream with pieces of chocolate and chantilly).

BARS/CAFÉS

NOTES

HACHETTE TRAVEL GUIDES

Titles available in this series:

HACHETTE VACANCES
Who better to write about France than the French?
A series of colourful, information-packed, leisure and activity guides
for family holidays by French authors. Literally hundreds of suggestions
for things to do and sights to see per title.

ROUTARD
Comprehensive and reliable guides offering insider advice for the
independent traveller.